HOW TO MAKE YOUR

IRA GROW

HOW TO MAKE YOUR IRA GROW

Investing under the New Tax Law

BY
PRISCILLA MEYER

GROVE PRESS INC. NEW YORK

Copyright © 1986 by Priscilla Meyer

All rights reserved.

No part of this book may be reproduced, stored in a retrieval system, or transmitted in any form, by any means, including mechanical, electronic, photocopying, recording or otherwise, without prior written permission of the publisher.

First Black Cat Edition 1986
First Printing 1986
ISBN: 0-394-62174-3
Library of Congress Catalog Card Number: 85-45937

Designed by Abe Lerner

Printed in the United States

GROVE PRESS, INC., 196 West Houston Street
New York, N.Y. 10014

5 4 3 2 1

CONTENTS

INTRODUCTION ... 1

PART I
Planning an IRA Around Your Financial Needs

1. HOW IRAS WORK ... 17
2. IRA INVESTING IS DIFFERENT ... 24
3. STRUCTURING YOUR IRA FOR PROFIT ... 29
4. DESIGNING AN IRA PORTFOLIO FOR YOUR NEEDS ... 42
5. STRATEGIES FOR YOUR IRA LIFE CYCLE ... 50
6. DO-IT-YOURSELF MARKET TIMING ... 56
7. NEW TAX LAW AND YOUR INVESTMENTS ... 62

PART II
Setting Up Your Investment Accounts

8. PICKING YOUR IRA ADMINISTRATOR ... 69
9. RUNNING YOUR OWN IRA ... 78
10. OTHER TAX SHELTER FOR RETIREMENT ... 84
11. TELEPHONE SWITCHING AND FUND FAMILIES ... 93
12. SELECTING BROKERS, BANKERS AND AGENTS ... 100
13. OPENING MARGIN ACCOUNTS ... 108
14. COMPARING RATES AND SERVICES ... 111
15. RESTITUTION: GETTING YOUR MONEY BACK ... 113

PART III
Ways to Earn Interest

16. RISK VERSUS REWARD ... 122
17. MONEY MARKET ACCOUNTS ... 128
18. FEDERAL GOVERNMENT SECURITIES ... 130
19. CORPORATE BONDS AND PREFERRED STOCK ... 134
20. TAX-EXEMPT SECURITIES ... 137

HOW TO MAKE YOUR IRA GROW

21. ACCUMULATION BONDS: ZEROS AND U.S. SAVINGS BONDS — 140
22. UNIT TRUSTS AND BOND MUTUAL FUNDS — 146

PART IV
Some Case Studies

23. SAVING FOR COLLEGE ON $1000 A YEAR — 154
24. RETIREMENT COMING UP AND UNPREPARED — 157
25. SINGLE, FLUSH AND GREEDY — 159

PART V
Playing the Stock Market

26. SCAMS AND WARNINGS — 165
27. EXCHANGE-LISTED STOCKS — 167
28. OVER-THE-COUNTER STOCKS — 172
29. HOW TO BUY AND SELL ON NEWS — 181
30. ARMCHAIR ARBITRAGE — 185
31. STOCK SHORTING — 190
32. HEDGING WITH OPTIONS — 194

PART VI
Some Investment Alternatives

33. COMMODITIES FUTURES AND OPTIONS — 200
34. COLLECTIBLES: THE MARKET INFLATION MADE — 204

PART VII
Technology and Your Investments

35. MANAGING INVESTMENTS BY HOME COMPUTER — 215
36. GETTING PRICE QUOTES AND RESEARCH — 217
37. TRADING SECURITIES BY COMPUTER — 222

GLOSSARY/INDEX — 224

Introduction

Just what exactly is an IRA? According to the Federal government, it is an Individual Retirement Arrangement that permits you to set aside before Federal income taxes up to $2000 of your annual salary to invest tax-free until you retire. As a result you pay less income tax on current income and your investment profits pile up more quickly than if they were taxed as they accrued to you.

I might have waited until a bit later in the book to give you that definition, but a recent conversation with a reasonably bright college graduate changed my mind. He thought IRAs were some form of special bank account, like a NOW account or a money market account.

That's not surprising since the initials IRA popularly stand for Individual Retirement Account. And you do set up an IRA by opening an account somewhere, or by investing in an annuity contract if you set up your IRA through an insurance company. But the account or annuity is merely the result of the government's Individual Retirement Arrangement.

Few people really understand IRA's, although Americans already have invested more than $200 billion in them and the tab is growing. Your decision to invest time and money in research is wise whether you are setting up your first IRA or even if you already have several, since it is simple to move IRAs from one type of investment to another or from institution to institution.

If you are like many people, your decision to start an

IRA will make you, for the first time, an investor. And like most first-time investors, you will want to know the best place to put your investment money right now and the best way to make your IRA grow over the years. Then you will want to know exactly how to set the mechanics into motion.

If this book took the usual approach, it would quickly caution you that there are no easy answers. Then it would admonish you against investment ventures that require extensive knowledge and monitoring, like the stock market (which over the years has had better average returns than any other major market).

The fact is that there *are* relatively safe ways to invest in almost anything, assuming you aren't dealing with fraud. As a little investor you can fare better in the stock market all by yourself than with the most costly investment advice. You can get a better return than most professional investment managers simply by playing "index" mutual funds that buy every stock in one of the broad market indexes like the Standard & Poor's 500 stocks. That takes no special research or sophistication.

And with a little additional effort, you can learn to select the stockmarket mutual fund, stock, bond, or commodities fund that is most likely to grow under varying market conditions. In fact, your little IRA may well outperform funds run by many professional investors.

For the past fifteen years I have been a financial journalist whose business it was to tell readers what is going on behind the scenes in the investment world—largely through the pages of the *Wall Street Journal*, *Forbes Magazine*, and the *New York Daily News*.

For most of that time my readers were investment professionals, or at least knowledgeable and experienced investors. However, with the rise of IRAs, it has become clear that the average intelligent person with little or no investment experience may now need to know how to cope in the complex area of individual investment. By using basic information sources, like this book, along with basic common sense, I believe an amateur investor can create a retirement fund for his or her family that will rival the investment performance of the pros.

Year after year professional money managers—of bank trust departments, brokerage firms, and mutual funds, for example—underperform the major market indexes on average. Why? For one thing, the competitive pros must attempt to anticipate big market turns, getting in ahead of time to catch the day or moment of the initial turn. When they are wrong, or even too early, losses result. Then too, professional research and money management are expensive and can cut into the potential return. What's more, big institutions have limitations on where they can invest, since few can afford to bother with less than $500,000 at a time. That means they must confine their investments to large stocks and securities.

You, as a little investor, have no such restrictions. And by making the right decisions about when to rely on professionals to do your investing for you and when to do it yourself, you can make your money grow even faster. For example, such high-risk investments as junk bonds—which are the riskiest bonds of all—become far less chancy when these issues are acquired by the hundred for high-yield mutual funds. Were you to buy a single junk bond, you'd run a real risk of a default, leaving you with nothing. But if you buy shares in a junk-bond mutual fund (they're usually called "high-yield" funds), it is likely that only one or two of the hundreds of issues held by the fund could default to reduce your return. It is in areas of such high risk and of complex securities that paying for professional management—through a mutual fund or otherwise—makes the most sense for the little investor. Not surprisingly, it is also in such areas that the pros perform best.

On the other hand, you don't need to pay a professional to help you select a super-safe Treasury Bond; you can place the order through a cut-rate discount broker. Nor do you need the protection of a mutual fund to limit risk. All such bonds are backed by the U.S. government and at any given time are virtually interchangeable in terms of risk and return.

What follows is a no-beating-around-the-bush look at what you can do to make your investment dollar grow faster than if you simply put it into a money market fund or bank Certificate of Deposit (although sometimes and for some people those are the right investments). This book will tell you what to do and how to do it, both inside your Individual Retirement Account (IRA) and out.

In the pages to come you will see that IRA investment rules are different than the rules that govern your investments outside your IRA (see Chapter 2). The basic purpose of IRA tax protection is to permit you to accumulate funds for your retirement that will grow faster than inflation eats up the value of your dollars.

You hear a lot of talk about IRAs ultimately making people into millionaires. While it is quite likely that some young couples starting out today may indeed accumulate more than $1 million in their IRA by the time they retire forty-five or fifty years from now, $1 million almost certainly will be worth substantially less by then than it is today. Assuming inflation continues at, say, 4.5% over the next forty-eight years, the value of a single dollar would drop to around 12 cents in today's money. As a result a million dollars in 2084 would be worth $120,000 in today's dollars.

It would be difficult to keep ahead of inflation in your effort to accumulate money for retirement without the tax-protection offered by the Federal government in the form of IRAs. For example, if you are in a 50% tax bracket, an interest yield of 8% before taxes will be reduced to 4% after taxes. This is growth at a slower rate even than many estimate for inflation in the coming decades.

By excluding money invested in an IRA and the interest it earns from current income taxation the full interest income is left free to compound at a rate exceeding inflation as the decades pass. To get an idea how fast your money will compound in an IRA see the tables at the end of this introductory section.

Chapter 6 will outline for you a simple investment strategy that will permit you to invest in the right place at the right time simply by checking interest rates in your newspaper once a week. It will spell out, investment by investment, where you should move your money during different market conditions. And it will tell you how to rate each specific investment for your own needs and how to modify that investment to serve your best interests.

Armed with this information you will be able to make an investment-by-investment survey, taking a close look at the mechanics, costs, and suitability of each investment possibility and the people and institutions that are out there to sell it to you. You will also learn something about commissions and fees and where it helps to shop for lower fees.

Traditionally, little investors have stumbled along, making the mistakes that permit professional traders to make the profits. With a little effort on your part, however, it doesn't need to be that way. Conventional wisdom is that individual investors are always the last to act. Their appearance in any investment market in great numbers is the signal for professional investors to withdraw. The big guys get out just as the little guys start getting in; the little investors, by buying, permit the professionals to get out by selling. Prices peak and the down cycle begins. Little investors are left once more holding the bag.

Information lag is at least partially to blame for this.

Most published investment advice available to the man-on-the-street comes after an investment cycle is well underway and is based on past experience—mutual funds that performed well in the preceding year, stocks that doubled in price over the last few months, or metals that tripled in price in the recent past. By the time word reaches the little investor most potential for profit is over. Professional traders attempt to anticipate such cycles near the bottom and ride them to the top. And while that strategy would be too risky for a small investor, there is no reason why he can't spot cycles already underway and cash in long before the end.

Adding to the effects of this information lag, the public is slow to change investment behavior. The average person for years kept his money in a conventional savings account, paying little attention to the 5.5% interest that gradually accumulated. When inflation raged in the 1970s, individuals discovered money market accounts, which gradually replaced savings accounts for the average small investor. But by the summer of 1982, when interest rates fell and the stock market suddenly rallied, individuals were left once again behind the times. They stuck to money market accounts.

At this writing, individuals are moving large amounts of money from the money market to the stock market. With this book and some thought and effort on your part, you should be able to spot major market shifts within weeks, or even days, after the professional traders do.

Time was when the small investors who were hurt were those who could best afford it. That is no longer so. With the advent of the IRA account the little investor has suddenly been put in charge of what can become huge amounts of money that will be significant to him and to his family in the future. Mistakes will be costly.

Today there's a new flood of self-proclaimed professionals attempting to cash in on what promises to be one of the biggest investment markets of all time. Five years ago, few had even heard of financial planners or computerized financial plans. Today the so-called financial planners are everywhere—with everyone from insurance agents to stockbrokers offering planning services biased in favor of whatever product they happen to sell. As an IRA investor you are suddenly being offered thousands of sophisticated investment products, accounts, and services that didn't even exist five years ago. Many are complex and some are downright fraudulent.

Obviously, most people don't have the time to become investment professionals just in order to manage their own IRAs. But, at the very least, an IRA investor can spend some time learning about the various types of investments and accounts that are possible, and developing some criteria for selecting a good professional advisor if he decides to turn this responsibility over to someone else.

This book is designed as a field guide for the amateur in the complex and sometimes dangerous world of investment. It is meant to help the investor who wants to see his IRA and other investments grow as safely and as rapidly as possible, but who can devote only limited time and attention to the task.

Welcome to the world of investment, and good luck!

COMPOUND INTEREST TABLES

Table 1. How much will you have for retirement? The following table tells how much you will have in the end if you put $1000 a year in your IRA or other tax-sheltered account at different rates of interest and over different periods of time. Multiply the number by 2 if you plan to put away $2000 a year, and by 4 if you are a married working couple with plans to put $4000 a year in your account.

HOW TO MAKE YOUR IRA GROW

Number of years	5%	7%	Interest rate 10%	12%	15%
1	1,050	$ 1,070	$ 1,100	$ 1,120	$ 1,150
5	5,802	6,150	6,710	7,100	7,750
10	13,207	14,790	17,520	19,640	23,350
15	22,657	26,890	34,940	41,730	54,720
20	34,719	43,490	62,190	79,530	116,020
30	69,760	100,890	183,090	277,620	528,920
40	126,839	213,890	496,690	892,730	2,195,020

3,594,835

Table 2. How fast does your dollar grow? This table shows how a one-time investment of $1000 grows over time at different rates of return.

Number of years	5%	7%	Interest rate 10%	12%	15%
5	1,276.3	$ 1,400	$ 1,610	$ 1,760	$ 2,010
10	1,628.8	1,970	2,590	3,110	4,050
15	2,078.0	2,760	4,180	5,470	8,140
20	2,653	3,870	6,720	9,650	16,370
30	4,322	7,610	17,450	29,960	66,210
40	7,040	14,980	45,260	93,050	267,000

PART I

Planning an IRA Around Your Financial Needs

FINANCIAL planning is the topic of the 1980s. Brokerage houses will sell you 100-page personalized financial plans for from $1000 to $10,000 or more. Merrill Lynch has a scaled-down version for the man-on-the-street at $250. American Express/IDS Financial Services has one for $100. And you can even buy a $50 computerized financial plan at many Sears Roebuck stores.

There's enough hoopla on the subject that anyone who doesn't have a financial plan is already feeling a bit guilty, like someone who missed their semiannual check-up at the dentist.

The truth is that you'll probably be better off in the long run if you think out a financial plan for yourself.

It won't hurt if you shell out $50 or $100 for one of the "personalized, computerized" plans that are available as a check on your own results, but you should understand what you are getting. The following points are important to consider:

1. **Most of these plans are sales tools for the products and services of the bank or brokerage house sponsoring the offer.** In short, your "personal" plan will be full of their products. For example, the computerized plan offered by Sears concludes its opening letter to the client by saying: "A copy of your Planner has been sent to your Dean Witter Account Executive. You will be contacted shortly to arrange a convenient time for a professional review and analysis. We have a whole team of professionally trained employees—Dean Witter in investments, Allstate in insurance and Coldwell Banker in real estate—ready to help you plan your own personal financial future." Dean Witter, Allstate, and Coldwell Banker are all Sears subsidiaries. By filling out the lengthy questionnaire about your own financial situation—assets, salaries, expenses and so forth—you provided the salesmen of these related companies with the sort of detailed information it would have been impossible for them to obtain otherwise. You may not mind, but you should know that is what happens.

2. **These plans are most useful for people who are on a salary of less than, say, $120,000 and who don't have tricky investments like tax shelter programs.** That's because most people have the same problems—too little income and the need to accumulate funds to send children to college, buy a house, or retire. People who are self-employed or whose assets are in unconventional investments will derive little benefit from these cookie-cutter plans. In a typical 24-page personal financial planner most of the typed information is general, while

the "personal" figures for income, potential savings, and goals are computer-inserted as in those mail order catalogs that say: "You, *Mrs. Jones*, may have won our $1 million sweepstakes!"

All this is not to pooh-pooh the solid information you can get from such a plan once you know the tricks. All of them will consider your current savings rate and your financial goals, throw in an inflation factor, and give you an idea of how much you must set aside today or year-by-year to reach your goals. For most people this figure is substantially more than they are currently setting aside. Generally, your IRAs are written into the formula although most such plans don't specify how your IRA money is invested.

Be certain you don't confuse financial plans with get-rich-quick schemes. More than a few scammers have business cards calling themselves financial planners and touting schemes suggesting you can double your money in three months. By comparison, valid financial plans are rather conservative and rarely specify any investments, certainly not high-risk, high-reward ones.

Some of the more expensive financial plans, particularly those prepared by people or companies not associated with other financial institutions with services to sell, do recommend specific types of investment for specific clients—tax-free unit trusts, high-yield stocks, specific tax shelters, and so forth. Such plans from independent planners generally cost in excess of $5000, and generally make sense only for people with incomes in excess of $150,000 a year. Even in such cases, the professional financial planner may be getting hidden kickbacks from institutions selling the products that are recommended. So even if you shell out $10,000 for an apparently independent financial plan you should be wary.

Also be careful of boilerplate financial advice, which tends to be confusing or misleading. Typically, a financial plan will recommend a certain portion of your investment portfolio go into inflation-hedging investments like stocks. Nothing could sound more logical, yet in stocks, for example, the big market rallies—the times you can make big money—come during periods of deflation. At the onset of periods of inflation, stock prices fall as interest rates rise. When inflation rages and rates are in the double-digit range, stock prices hit their low point.

The trick to making your IRA grow is being in the right investments at the right time and that's what this book is all about. So as an alternative to hiring a financial planner or buying a personal financial plan, you may decide to forget the forms, estimates of liquid and actual net worth, and computer calculations. Instead, sit down one evening with a pencil and yellow tablet to do some serious thinking. Several good books on financial planning are available to give you guidance along the way.

SHOULD YOU HAVE AN IRA?

Believe it or not, IRAs aren't for everyone. Today more than 40 million Americans have more than $200 billion in IRAs. But that doesn't necessarily mean that all those who don't have IRAs have slipped up. For example, a young couple with a relatively low income of, say, $12,000 a year might be wise to bypass even small IRAs of $500 or less. True, that $500, invested tax-free in an IRA today at 12%, would double six times to $32,000 over the next thirty-six years. But there are offsetting considerations. For one thing, at that salary investment income outside the IRA would be taxed at the relatively low rate of 15%, even under the proposed flat tax. That means the effective interest rate after taxes would be 10.2%—permitting the money to double every 7 years. And by investing outside an IRA the couple would retain constant access to their money in case, for example, the refrigerator broke down or they had an unexpected baby. If they had been collecting the full 12% in an IRA and needed to withdraw that money they would have had to pay a 10% fine on every dollar they withdrew, and that fine could increase to 20% under coming tax reform. Either way they would have to pay income tax on the withdrawn money—if it was from inside an IRA the tax would be paid in the year of withdrawal; outside the IRA it would have been paid in the year the money was earned. This means that if their income had increased before the withdrawal they would have to pay a higher tax when the funds were withdrawn from the IRA.

AN IRA INCOME TEST

When are you ready to start an IRA? Here are a few guidelines:

First, pay off any high-interest installment loans or charge accounts. Most revolving credit cards charge at an annual rate of about 18%, but some charge as much as 22%. This is reverse compounding. Compounding interest at, say, 12% permits your IRA investment to double every six years; compounded interest that you pay on installment loans can double the cost of your loan every 8 years (assuming you are in a 50% tax bracket and can use half of the interest as a tax deduction). The cost will double every four years when you lose the right to deduct the interest, as is likely under the new tax law.

You must, of course, pay off these accounts with after-tax dollars; meanwhile your IRA would be funded with fatter pre-tax dollars. As a result it makes sense to retain any low-cost loans—from your credit union, for example, or against the cash value of your life insurance policy. Your potential to generate such low-cost loans in the future can also be a factor in your decision to start an IRA today.

Second, make certain you have adequate money at hand for emergencies. How much? One rule of thumb is about three months worth of income. This money can be in a money market account and earning interest; but it should not be put into an IRA where you must pay penalty fees and go through red tape to remove it. Nor should it go into a Certificate of Deposit or any other type of investment where you must pay penalties for removing sums before the maturity date. Your emergency money must be instantly available to you.

Third, plan ahead for large expenditures that you will want to make before your retirement years. Such could include the down payment on a house or college expenses for you or your children. Under most circumstances you should estimate when you will need this money and how much you will need, then set aside enough to accumulate the amounts you will need before setting up your IRAs. Such special funds could be put into a money market account or you could be more venturesome, selecting different kinds of investments under different market conditions as outlined in Chapter 6. And, under some circumstances, you may even want to accumulate some or all of this money in your IRAs.

Now, if you have any money for investment left, you are well situated to start an IRA. The size will depend on the amount of money you have available, up to the government's annual limits of $2000 for a working individual.

Besides using IRAs to save for retirement you might consider using your IRA as suggested above, to accumulate money for large long-term purchases, particularly for the down payment on a first house or for college educations. Under the new tax law, penalties for withdrawing IRA money for these two purposes will remain at 10%, while other premature withdrawals would be penalized at 20%. Of course, this maneuver could actually cost you money if you set up the IRA when you were in a low tax bracket and removed it when you were in a higher tax bracket since you pay taxes on this money when you remove it. The computations are complicated, but here is a rough idea of how many years of tax-free compounding in your IRA are needed to offset the 10% tax penalty and make such use for your IRA profitable:

Years of IRA compounding needed to offset 10% penalty

tax bracket	interest rate			
	@ 8% for: (no. of yrs.)	@ 10% for: (no. of yrs.)	@ 12% for: (no. of yrs.)	@ 14% for: (no. of yrs.)
25%	8	6	5	5
35%	7	6	5	4
50%	6	5	5	4

In the course of saving for such large expenditures, you could find yourself short of money to continue building your fund. You might then consider borrowing—if you have access to low-cost loans from life insurance policies or credit unions—to set up your IRA.

One advantage to setting up IRAs even in the lean early years is that later, when you may have plenty of money to invest, you may want to exceed the $2000 annual limit. If you borrow now at a low rate, particularly if the loan is arranged in a way that doesn't demand an immediate schedule of repayment, you may be able to pay back the loan in the future when you have more money, in effect creating a larger IRA than if you had skipped IRA startups in the early years.

Later in your career, when you are in the happy situation of having more money to invest than you can use up in your $2000 IRA quota, you will also want to invest outside your IRA. It is here you will be able to make the fullest use of this book—possibly dabbling in high-risk, high-reward, speculative areas in the early years and later moving into more conservative investments such as tax-free municipal bonds to protect your profits.

I
How IRAs Work

To qualify under Federal law, you must open IRA accounts with financial institutions that are recognized by the Internal Revenue Service as trustees or custodians for IRAs. Institutions qualify by following model rules set up by the IRS, and most large banks, brokerage houses, and insurance companies are equipped to offer IRA accounts. The paperwork necessary for you to open such an IRA is minimal and is handled by the institution—bank, brokerage house, mutual fund manager, or insurance company—that you select. You don't even need to fill out a special form at tax time. However, you cannot open an ordinary account with one of these institutions, then simply fill out some forms at year-end and proclaim it your IRA.

Over the years you may set up many IRAs of different types with different institutions. Some you may run yourself, making your own decisions on what to buy and when to move your money from one type of investment to another. Others may be run by IRA trustees, who can be a bank, savings and loan, or other institution. You can, year after year, continue putting money into one continuous IRA, or you can set up several IRAs each year, ending up, if you want, with forty or fifty of them.

Government guidelines limit the total amount that you may set aside in your IRAs each year—$2000 for an individual, $4000 for a married, working couple. The money going into your IRA must come from your salary, unless you are a non-working spouse, and you can't set

IRAs up for your unsalaried children. There is, however, no minimum age for IRA-holders, and if and when a child begins to earn a salary, he can have his own IRA. As a practical matter, of course, it would not make much sense for most children to shelter income in an IRA, since their salaries and potential tax liabilities tend to be low. On the other hand, a child model or actor generating a large salary might want to put some of it aside, tax free, in an IRA.

Here is a look at some basic IRA rules:

Age requirements. While there is no minimum age to open an IRA, there is a maximum age. You may not open an IRA if you are over seventy and one-half years old and you also may not contribute to an existing IRA after that. However, the younger spouse of such an over age person can still initiate and contribute to an IRA until he or she reaches the age limit.

As for withdrawals, you may start taking out money without penalty at age fifty-nine and one-half and you *must* start taking money out of your IRA by the time you are seventy and one-half and continue to make regular withdrawals, taking all of it out by the time you turn eighty-two and one-half (in twelve and one-tenth years) if you are a man, or eighty-five and one-half (fifteen years) if you are a woman. The difference results from the longer life expectancy for women. The schedule is spelled out in IRS Publication 590, which is available at most public libraries or from IRS forms distribution centers in most states. It is also spelled out in IRS tax form 5329—Return for Individual Retirement Arrangement Taxes—which you must file annually at tax time once you begin withdrawals. This is also the form you file if you are required to pay any IRA penalties.

If you delay past the seventy and one-half age deadline you will be penalized with a 50% tax on what you should have taken out under the withdraw schedule.

PLANNING AN IRA AROUND YOUR FINANCIAL NEEDS

Methods of withdrawal. When you retire you may select from among several methods of withdrawal. One choice is to take everything you have accumulated in your IRA in one lump sum. The problem with this is that you will have to pay taxes on the total amount that year as if that were your salary. A second choice is to arrange a schedule of payments to be made to yourself, using the IRS life expectancy tables for minimum annual withdrawals and paying taxes on your withdrawals as if that were your annual salary. A third choice is to withdraw all or part of your IRA in a lump sum and invest the money immediately in a lifetime annuity purchased from an insurance company. With that choice you and your spouse will receive regular and guaranteed annual payments as long as either of you lives. If you live beyond your statistical life expectancy, you end up collecting more than your initial investment; in any case, the annuity ends with your death (or that of a surviving spouse) and your heirs receive nothing.

If an annuity is your option, you can generally expect to get an annual payment of around $100 for each $1000 you invest. For an annual benefit of $25,000, for example, you would need to purchase an annuity costing roughly $250,000. See the Compound Interest Tables at the end of the Introduction to get an idea of how much money you must put into an IRA each year, the rate of interest you must obtain, and the number of years you must invest at varying interest rates to end up with $250,000 or whatever amount you determine you will need over your retirement years.

You may decide to combine a lifetime annuity with other interest-bearing investments as assurance that you will have something other than Social Security if you live to, say, 110 years old. You can also use an Individual Retirement Annuity from an insurance company to accumulate your retirement funds over the years. In that case you can select either regular payments over your lifetime or the lump sum distribution when it is time for withdrawals to begin.

Maximum and minimum size. Under the new tax law individuals may set aside a maximum of $2000 a year—that's the amount of money you put into your IRA and not any interest that accumulates during the year from your deposits. Married couples may each set up a $2000 IRA each year if both are working and earning more than $2000 a year. Under the proposed tax changes the $4000 limit would be extended to married couples with only one spouse working outside the house; currently, the IRA limit for such a couple is $2250 annually. With this one exception, no one can put more money into an IRA than his annual salary, including income from commissions and fees. Income from other sources, such as investments, doesn't qualify.

You can be penalized for putting too much money into an IRA in a given year. That can happen if you open IRAs at several institutions and your deposits in any one year total more than $2000. You are also in violation if you use a monthly contribution plan and one too many payments is credited to your IRA in a given year. The institutions with which you have your IRAs aren't held responsible for these violations; you are. There is a 6% tax on each dollar over $2000 that you deposit and the penalty isn't deductible for tax purposes.

Technically there is no minimum size for an IRA, although most institutions won't set up IRA accounts for less than $500.

Moving your money. You may move some or all of your IRA money from one institution to another as often as you want, as far as the government is concerned. Some institutions impose withdrawal penalties and other roadblocks, however, so it's important to read your IRA agreement carefully before signing it. The government requires the institution to make full disclosure of the terms of your account, including any withdrawal penalties.

Although you can't start an IRA with securities you already own—you must have cash—you can often transfer IRA securities between IRA institutions. In general, it is up to the receiving institution whether or not it considers your securities acceptable. If not, you will have to convert your securities into cash for transferral, paying out money for both sale and repurchase fees. Currently such fees can't be paid with money outside your IRA, so they cut into your valuable IRA funds, but several brokers are attempting to get the IRS to reinterpret this stipulation. Fees paid to an IRA trustee for acting as your custodian can be paid with outside money.

Certain types of investment, like bank Certificates of Deposit, carry penalties for liquidation before they run full term. With CDs you usually must forfeit six-months' worth of interest.

Over a short term you can take all or part of the money out of your IRA as cash and use it for personal expenditures or anything else, but you must redeposit the funds into an IRA within 60 days or pay a penalty on the money that you have withdrawn. You may only do this once every 12 months under the IRS rules.

Under the new tax law, if you withdraw any funds from your IRA prematurely you may have to pay a 20% penalty—up from 10% under current law. Then you must pay taxes on the withdrawn funds as if they were investment income. But, even under the new law, if you remove funds prematurely to finance college educations, to purchase a home as a primary residence, or to replace unemployment benefits the old 10% penalty would still apply.

Pension Rollover. You may rollover into a personal IRA any money that you get as a distribution of pension funds. You may do this whether you collect the pension money when you retire or because you change jobs. The same rules that apply to institution-to-institution transfer of IRA money (see **Moving your money,** p. 20) apply to pension-to-IRA rollovers.

What the IRA trustee must tell you. Under law, when you open an IRA account the institution that will act as trustee or custodian must give you a disclosure statement about your program. It is important for you to read it immediately and completely even though it will appear to be full of legalese and gobbledygook. This document provides you with a projection of the growth in value of your IRA investment. If you have invested at a predetermined rate of interest—as in a certificate of deposit— the institution must show you how much money you would have if you were to withdraw your funds at the end of five years and when you reach the ages of sixty, sixty-five, and seventy. It must also show your current earnings rate and the terms on which the projection is based. The sponsor must also disclose any charges, such as sales commissions, made against your IRA payments and how annual earnings will be calculated. And the disclosure form must also detail when and how you may cancel the IRA program, along with penalties and other tax effects of premature withdrawals.

Currently you will find that many institutions aren't charging administration fees, but reserve the right to begin charging them in the future. You should watch your mail carefully for such notices. In an effort to drum up new accounts many institutions are waiving administration fees for the moment, but such fees are likely in the future. The institution must notify you within thirty days if such a change is made.

If, after reading the disclosure statement, you decide to cancel your account, the IRS gives you seven days to reach such a decision. If you cancel before seven days— do it both by phone and letter to be on the safe side

—you cannot be charged any sales commissions, administrative expenses, or for any changes in market value of your IRA investment.

Death or divorce. All taxable alimony received by a divorced spouse under a divorce decree or separate maintenance will be treated as compensation and thus will be eligible for an IRA. If you inherit an IRA from a deceased spouse you generally have several options, including rolling it over into your own IRA—wherein these funds are governed by the same rules as your own—or keeping it separate—wherein it continues to operate on your spouse's timetable even though he or she is dead. If you inherit an IRA from someone other than your spouse, you probably can't roll it over into your own. The rules applying to IRAs passed to you by death or divorce are spelled out in IRS publication 590, which may be obtained from the Internal Revenue Service.

2

IRA Investing Is Different

Investing inside your IRA is significantly different from investing outside of it. In order to make the best use of this government-provided tax shelter, it is important that you understand and plan in accordance with the IRA features discussed below:

Earnings inside your IRA will ultimately be taxed at the full investment income rate. Before tax reform the rate amounted to 50% in the maximum brackets. The rule applies whether the IRA earnings come from dividends as investment income (which would be taxed at the full rate whether outside or inside the IRA) or long-term capital gains (which would be taxed outside—but not inside—at a lower rate—20% in the maximum bracket before reform.)

Investment income includes what you earn in your money market account, as interest on Certificates of Deposit and as dividends from stocks and bonds. By comparison, capital gains or losses come from changes in the value of your investments. If you buy a non-dividend-paying common stock for $10 a share and sell it for $15 a share you will have a $5-a-share capital gain. If you sell the investment in less than six months and a day, you must pay the higher short-term capital gains tax, which is the same as your income tax rate and your rate for investment income. However, if you hold the investment longer than that, you qualify for the lower long-term capital gains tax, which currently is 40% of your tax rate (To figure the tax rate you would pay—in the top 50% tax bracket, for example—you multiply .40 × .50, obtaining a 20% tax rate.)

Under tax reform it's likely that the top maximum bracket will come down to somewhere between 35% and 38% from its current 50% level. That will reduce the tax advantage of long-term capital gains over other forms of earnings from investment since the long-term capital gains tax is likely to remain at a maximum of 20% under a new formula. But the difference will still be significant, leaving you with a strong incentive to use the IRA tax shelter as protection for income that would be most highly taxed on the outside.

Losses shown inside your IRA not only eat up valuable tax-protected IRA dollars, but put you at a tax disadvantage. Outside your IRA, losses can be written off for tax purposes against capital gains and investment income in current and future years. Specifically, short-term capital losses—the losses you take when you sell a security less than six months and a day after you bought it and get less than you paid for it—can be used to offset taxes on any capital gains you obtain outside your IRA. After subtracting out your capital gains, if you still have a net loss, you can write up to $3000 off against investment income or ordinary income. And if your losses exceed this 3000 limit, you can carry them over into another tax year and write them off against gains or income in the future. Writeoffs as a result of long-term capital losses work much the same way—but since long-term capital gains are taxed at a lower rate, you must divide long-term capital losses in half before you can write them off against other forms of income.

In no case, however, can capital losses that occur

inside your IRA be used for tax writeoffs, either inside or outside your IRA. As a result it makes sense to take the smallest possible risks of losses inside your IRA, and do your speculating on the outside.

Ironically, some wealthy investors use their IRAs for fast in-and-out stock trading and speculation since they can avoid paying taxes at the higher short-term capital gains rate (50% in the top bracket). In such cases they are willing to forego writeoffs for losses in exchange for the high tax-free profits that they hope to obtain. The biggest current disadvantage to this—if you don't need your IRA for security—is that trading fees and commissions must be paid from the funds in your IRA, cutting sharply into any tax-sheltered profits.

Fees and commissions can make a substantial difference in an IRA. Not only can brokerage fees and commissions and front-end loads on mutual funds and other investment programs eat up your tax-sheltered dollars, since they must be paid from your actual IRA money, but these fees can't be written off for tax purposes. On the other hand, fees charged by the custodian or trustee who administers your IRA can be written off for tax purposes. You are billed outside your IRA and you don't pay administration fees with precious tax-sheltered money.

Obviously it makes sense to avoid the type of IRA investment that comes with big front-end sales fees or trading costs—or, at the very least, to shop carefully for a discount broker. Even the cheapest discount brokers often are able to set up IRAs for you. (See Chapter 12 on shopping for a broker.)

There are some things you can't do with an IRA that are quite legitimate with non-IRA investments. For one thing you can't use your IRA investments as security for a loan; for another, you can't borrow funds from your IRA for more than sixty days, and that means it is illegal, for example, to use your IRA for your own home mortgage. You can put real estate or property into your IRA—if you can find something that you can buy in $2000 chunks or if you use rollover or accumulated IRA money—but you can't be the one to sell that property to your own IRA. You can also pay yourself something for managing your own IRA (see Chapter 9 on self-run IRAs) but you can run afoul of the IRS if you receive "unreasonable compensation" for managing it.

What happens if you violate any of these restrictions? For one thing, IRAs set up in the year of the violation will no longer count as IRAs, and the money held therein will be treated as taxable income. You probably will also have to pay a 10% penalty (20% under the new law), since removal of IRA status would cause that year's IRAs to qualify as "premature distributions." Similar penalties would apply if any of your IRA money were used to pay for insurance or if you were to borrow against your IRA annuity contract.

It makes sense to invest IRA money early in the year. Invest at the soonest possible moment—January 1 of any year—rather than waiting until the last possible moment—tax time (April 15) of the following year. The difference is more than one full year of interest—which will amount to $200 if you invest your full $2000 at 10%. That may not sound like much now, but with your money doubling every seven or so years, that $200 in extra interest would grow into $12,800 in forty-two years.

After giving due consideration to these IRA investment rules, many investors conclude that the best IRA investments are those where there is little danger of capital losses, few if any trading or sales fees, and where income that would be most highly-taxed outside an IRA can benefit from IRA tax-protection. Investments which best meet these criteria are the Certificates of Deposit that you buy from your bank or money market accounts—

either no-load ones from mutual fund families or those from a bank or thrift institution. Long-term bonds that you hold to maturity and insurance company Individual Retirement Annuities also have desirable features for IRAs, although both can involve fees that must come from your IRA.

3
Structuring Your IRA for Profit

This chapter contains a laundry list of investments that are generally most suitable for your IRA, based on the IRA investment differences outlined in the preceding chapter. You can certainly put other investments in your IRA—as the rest of this book will explain—but you should have good reasons for doing so.

INVESTMENTS THAT BEST USE IRA TAX SHELTER

The investments that make the fullest use of IRA advantages are those that show no potential for loss of your principal (your initial investment), that earn investment income rather than short-term capital gains, and that charge a minimum of fees of the sort that must come directly from your IRA. All such investments make use of compounded interest, and an important factor in comparing such investments is the frequency with which the interest is compounded. Sometimes you will see CDs and other investments advertised that pay a specified annual interest rate—say 10.5%—and then show another figure—say 10.78%—for yield. This is your clue that the rate is compounded more frequently than once a year. If it is compounded quarterly, for example, you are earning interest in the second quarter of the year on interest credited to your account at the end of the first quarter.

Can frequency of compounding make a big difference over the years? If you invested $2000 a year in IRAs for thirty years at 10%, you would end up with $363,885 if interest were compounded annually, $405,880 if it were compounded quarterly, and $421,700 if it were compounded daily. In this example, the difference between daily compounding and annual compounding is $57,815, with daily compounding creating 16% more income than yearly compounding. The longer your money compounds, the greater the difference. Thus in comparing CDs, zero-coupon bonds, and money market accounts it is better to look at projected yield—which includes current interest plus any compounding—than pure interest rates.

Certificates of Deposit. When you buy a CD you agree to leave a specified amount of money on deposit with your bank, savings and loan institution, or credit union for a predetermined period, usually from three months to five years. Along the way you collect interest at a predetermined rate—usually higher than that paid on your money market account deposits. When your CD matures you get all your money back or you may roll it over into another CD and start again. CDs may be purchased from the banks that issue them and some big discount brokers associated with banks will also sell them. Administration fees for maintaining IRA accounts holding CDs are generally low or nonexistent and they do not require much attention—you have nothing to do after purchase but decide whether or not to roll over the CD when it matures.

One note of caution: If you withdraw your money from the CD before it matures, you can be hit with big penalties—about six-months' worth of interest is the usual charge made by banks. Assuming you hold the CD to maturity, however, your original investment can't shrink as a result of market activity and it is Federally insured up to $100,000 if you make sure to buy it from a Federally insured institution.

Money market accounts with banks or no-load mutual fund families. Such accounts invest in Treasury Bills, large-sized Certificates of Deposit, and commercial paper—all short-term money market investments that mature in less than a year. As each investment matures, the bank or fund reinvests the money in another money market instrument, so the investor is spared the inconvenience of rolling over these investments or even thinking much about them.

In general, money market accounts are the most convenient of all forms of investment. They tend to pay interest at rates slightly lower than you would get for a two-to-five-year CD, although you can shop for higher rates among the money market funds, giving up a little safety to obtain more return. The safest are money market deposit accounts run by Federally insured banks, which are backed by $100,000 insurance for each account, and those that invest only in such securities as Treasury Bills that are backed by the Federal government. Of course, such types tend to have lower returns than money market funds investing in commercial paper or short-term IOUs issued by corporations (see Chapter 19).

In shopping around for money market mutual fund shares be aware that some funds charge an up-front load, or sales charge and that brokerage firms charge you commissions for your purchase of money market fund shares. These fees, remember, come directly out of your tax-sheltered IRA dollars.

Money market securities. You can also go directly into the money market and buy Treasury Bills—which are sold in maturities ranging from thirteen weeks to a year—and other money market securities. In general, though, these securities are sold in denominations of

$10,000 and more, making such direct purchases impractical for most IRAs.

Long-term bonds that you can hold to maturity. If you can hold a five-to-thirty-year bond in your account until it matures, you will get back all of your initial investment without showing any capital losses; you will also be able to collect the predetermined amount of interest, either when the bond matures or along the way. To do this, if you are anywhere near retirement age, you must select bonds with maturity schedules that coincide with your needs for withdrawing your IRA funds. Let's say, for example, that you intend to retire nine years from now and want to withdraw your money over the following ten years. You will want to buy an assortment of bonds—which generally come in $1000 denominations—that mature in ten years, eleven years, twelve years, and so forth. This is relatively simple to do if, instead of buying newly issued bonds, you make your purchases in the secondary market where previously issued bonds trade just like stocks. There, you can select bonds that mature exactly when you want them to mature.

Even if a particular bond is selling in the secondary market at a price higher than its original price, which is the amount you will get when you redeem it, you will not lose money if you hold it to maturity. That is because bond prices rise as interest rates fall. Dividend payments that you collect from your bonds will be higher than the return you would have been able to get if you had purchased newly issued bonds of the same quality on the same date. You will make up the difference with higher dividend payments (which you should reinvest as soon as they are paid). Let's say, hypothetically, a company issues ten-year bonds that will pay $100 a year in dividends for each $1000 bond, or 10%. Several years later, when you go to buy that bond in the secondary market, interest rates, generally, have fallen. Thus, if you were to purchase a new bond of comparable quality you would only get 8% or $80 a year. As a result the return, or yield, on the old bond you want to buy in the secondary market drops to 8%. This change is not reflected in the amount each bond will pay in dividends, which remains at $100 a year per bond per year. Instead, the market price that you must pay for the bond in the secondary market rises to, say, $1050 per bond. But, offsetting the higher price you pay for the bond, the dividend you receive will be $100 a year rather than $80 a year, permitting you, in effect, to get back part of your principal along the way. You collect the rest when the bond matures, producing the same result as if you had purchased, at the going yield of 8%, a newly issued bond at $1000, or par. (When a $1000 face amount bond is selling for $1000 it is selling at par.)

The case above illustrates how you can get back your total principal and have it yield, over the life of the bond, whatever amount was predetermined. But remember, this example only applies to *buying* your bond in the secondary market, not *selling* it there. If you must sell your bond in the secondary market, the price you get is totally dependent on interest rates at the time, and if rates have gone up since you bought the bond, you will have to show a capital loss. It is for this reason that shares in long-term mutual funds—which in general behave like the actual bonds—are less suitable than the bonds themselves for your IRA if you are anywhere near retirement and the need to redeem them. At no time do your bond fund shares mature, and you could end up showing a capital loss when you redeem your shares in much the same way that you can lose by selling bonds in the secondary market. Bond fund shares bought well before retirement are another matter, however, since, presumably, if the market price of the shares drops below the amount you paid, you can hold onto them until they recoup.

What types of bonds and bond funds are most suitable for IRAs? Here is a look at the main choices:

Government bonds. Primarily made up of Treasury Bonds issued to finance the U.S. Government, these are the safest and pay the lowest interest of all long-term bonds, although the rate is usually 2 or 3 percentage points higher than the return in your money market account. The smallest denomination you can buy from the U.S. Treasury through your bank or broker or in the secondary market is $5,000. For smaller denominations, you must turn to long-term bond mutual funds, which usually have minimums of $1000 or less (see Chapter 18). Or you can buy government securities in the form of *zero-coupon bonds*, which usually come in small denominations as they are specially packaged by stockbrokers for IRAs. If you intend to hold the bond to maturity there is no reason not to buy zeros, which often pay as much as one percentage point more than the underlying Treasury Bonds. That's because interest earned by zeros is credited to your account but not actually redeemed until your zero matures—which permits the institution that sold you the zero to make use of interest payments made by the underlying Treasury Bonds until they must be redeemed (see Chapter 21).

Government agency issues. Bonds sold to finance government agencies or to make mortgages under the government umbrella for agencies such as the Government National Mortgage Association (Ginnie Mae) usually pay about one percentage point more than Treasury Bonds. The actual Ginnie Maes can only be purchased in $10,000 denominations and larger, but $1000 units can be bought through Ginnie Mae mutual funds and Ginnie Mae unit trusts sold by stockbrokers. The most convenient way to invest is to buy the mutual funds, which continuously reinvest the hodge-podge of interest and principal payments that result from a Ginnie Mae. A possible disadvantage of this investment is that the mutual fund shares don't mature. Shares of unit trusts, which represent joint ownership by a number of investors in a specific batch of Ginnie Mae certificates, do mature, but often have the disadvantage that big fees are written into your purchase price—8% to 20% of your investment—that in effect come from your precious IRA dollars. (see Chapter 18).

Corporate Bonds. Companies issue bonds in a wide range of quality and maturities. In general, IRA investors should stick to grades of A or better (see Chapter 16). Since corporate bonds come in $1000 denominations, it makes sense to buy the actual bond—assuming you stick to bonds that are high rated. This is particularly true if you are nearing retirement and want to select a maturity date. If you buy them from a stockbroker or discount broker, you will pay commissions that are comparable to those you pay for buying and selling stocks. But if all you intend to do is buy the bond and hold it until maturity, this commission—which must be paid from your IRA—will amount to far less than the management fees you would pay if you invested in a mutual fund holding corporate bonds. For the purposes of your IRA, however, you will want any dividends to be reinvested in your IRA as soon as they are paid. Thus, you must determine whether that service is offered by your broker and then compare the cost of the brokerage service to the management fees of the mutual fund, which automatically reinvests dividends and may charge in the range of 1%–2% a year, or $10 to $20 per $1000 worth of assets.

An alternative, particularly if you want to select a maturity date—which isn't possible in a mutual fund—is to buy corporate bonds that are issued as zero-coupon bonds. In such cases it is the company issuing the bond rather than your stockbroker that retains use of your interest as it accumulates. If you invest in this type of security, it is important to select zero-coupon corporates that are high rated by the agencies, and you may want to look into the soundness of the issuing company.

In selecting bond investments you should not, under any circumstances, put municipal or other tax-exempt bonds into your IRA; nor should you attempt to put U.S. Savings Bonds in your IRA. Both offer built-in tax benefits to an investor apart from the IRA tax advantages and pay significantly lower interest than securities without these tax benefits.

Individual Retirement Annuities. Work pretty much like bank Certificates of Deposit, except that you buy them from insurance companies and they are riddled with penalties for withdrawal, which would come right out of your IRA. These are not to be confused with ordinary annuities (which you also buy from insurance companies) that offer you a set income for life for a basic one-time premium. The retirement annuities were created just for IRAs; they offer you a fixed rate of interest and guarantee your principal year by year. If you don't like the interest rate offered in a particular year, you can skip contributing to the IRA that year, but you can't withdraw funds already deposited without incurring all the penalties. Insurance companies have not been wildly successful in selling these retirement annuities, perhaps because their insurance agents tend to get paid a flat $20 commission for selling them to you.

There is another variety of retirement annuity, the variable retirement annuity, which works more like a mutual fund switching family. With this type of annuity your principal isn't guaranteed, and the funds—be they in the stock, bond or money market category—should be evaluated as investments in their own right.

SPECIAL SITUATIONS

That pretty much concludes the list of investments most able to make use of the tax benefits—and skirt the shortcomings—of IRAs. Unfortunately, there are certain market conditions where none of these securities make particularly good investments. For the purpose of coping with such markets—which include long periods of low interest and periods where interest rates are on the rise— here are a few suggested investments which would do well in such markets, even if there is some potential for capital losses. All are proposed as temporary ways to invest portions of your IRA money and not as long-term investments.

When interest rates are low and falling. From the standpoint of your IRA, stocks and stockmarket mutual funds are a less than ideal investment since even the safest ones dip in price when interest rates are on the rise. If you have to sell when such conditions prevail, you can incur unwanted and unusable capital losses in your IRA. To state this is not to knock stocks in general for little investors. Over the last few decades financial returns on stocks, including prices and dividends, have averaged 9.5% to investors, a respectable return. The problem is that this rate of return masks a history of big profits and big losses along the way. Outside your IRA you could take the profits as long-term capital gains, paying taxes at rates of 20% or lower. And you could write the losses off for tax purposes against profits and gains shown then or in future years. But inside your IRA the losses would eat up valuable tax-sheltered IRA dollars and be otherwise useless.

There is one time however, when you may want to consider moving some of your IRA money into the stock market or stockmarket mutual funds. That is when interest rates are relatively low and continuing downward. At such a point the return on newly issued interest-rate bearing investments is starting to look disappointing, and stock prices are strongly on the rise. However, any such investment move should be temporary, and you should switch over to a money market fund other low-risk investment the minute interest rates show any sign of rising. Stock prices tend to plummet at such times, and it is better to get out of the stock market with your IRA money intact than to risk waiting too long.

Don't be fooled, incidentally, by the common though specious advice of some mutual fund salesmen that you will make the best profits by purchasing a predetermined amount of shares each month—say $100 worth—regardless of whether share prices are going up or down. The case is argued like this: When stock prices rise, the value of your mutual fund holdings rises; when they fall, you can buy more shares for your money. But the argument can also be reversed as follows: When stock prices fall, the value of your holdings drop; when they rise, you are buying fewer shares for your money. So don't be taken in.

Quite simply, you don't want to be in the stock market when there is any danger of big losses. Period. Of course, you will have to pay the brokerage commissions from your IRA dollars to get in and then out of the stock market, but even small gains in your portfolio should more than cover that cost. As an alternative course of action, if you have invested through a family of no-load mutual funds that offers several stock market alternatives, you should be able to switch into a stockmarket fund and back to a money market fund at no extra cost to you at all.

When interest rates continue low. Once interest rates stop dropping, the value of your stock market holdings will either level out or climb at a slower pace. Meanwhile, the most suitable investments for your IRA—Certificates of Deposit, for example—are paying low interest. In such circumstances you can continue to hold onto your common stocks or you can increase income coming into your IRA by switching to stocks that pay high dividends. With such stocks you should be able to equal the return of high-grade corporate bonds, and at the same time, the market price of your shares could rise a bit as well.

Mutual fund families offer high-yield funds composed of such stocks or of a combination of high-yield stocks and bonds. Such families may also offer bond funds with even higher yields that are composed primarily of socalled junk bonds. In a period of sustained low interest rates, when Treasury Bonds are paying less than 10%, such funds can pay 14% and more. With such funds there is a risk that some of the bond issuers will withhold dividends or even collapse; however, over the short term such an unhappy event would probably do no more than lower your yield. Under no circumstances, however, should you hold individual junk, or super high-yield, bonds in your IRA, since, in case of collapse, you could lose not only the interest but all of your principal as well.

When you are following this investment strategy, you must constantly watch interest rates so that you can switch immediately out of all stocks and high-yield bonds and funds the minute interest rates show a hint of rising. Remember, if rates rise, the value of these holdings will plunge, and it is better—in an IRA anyway—to be safe than sorry.

When interest rates are low and rising. This is the most difficult market of all, since the market prices of both stocks and bonds tumble—a matter of little difference to you if you have purchased bonds that you intend to hold to maturity. For new IRA purchases, however, this is an easy place to go wrong. Under the circumstances it makes sense to put all or most of your IRA money into money market accounts or into short-term investments like three-month CDs or Treasury Bills. There you will earn little money while rates are still low, but you at least won't lost any of your principal.

There is one gambit you might try with part—say 5%—of your IRA money in an attempt to get a better return for your total IRA portfolio in such a market. The idea is to hedge your portfolio with some investments that increase in value as inflation heats up. Unfortunately, such investments tend to be risky, and unwanted losses can result. On the other hand, values can rise so sharply that a small investment of 5% of your portfolio can add several percentage points to your total return, offsetting low returns in the money market.

What investments tend to rise in price during such markets? Commodities, particularly gold, and real estate—two very tricky areas from the standpoint of your IRA. You can, however, buy shares in gold funds through many mutual fund families. These funds buy shares in gold-producing companies and gold contracts, both of which rise along with the price of gold. You also might sell short stock or bond market indexes in the options market, although this involves risking 100% of the money that you invest in them (see Chapter 31).

As to real estate, there are several very different kinds of investments. To ride the market of increasing rates, you particularly want investment partnerships or shares of companies that invest in income-producing properties which they own, collecting rents that come to you as dividends or investment income. You can do this in the stock market by buying shares of equity real estate investment trusts (REITs).

REITs. There are three kinds of REITs—equity, mortgage, and combined, and you can quickly determine the nature of a REIT by asking for a copy of its annual report or going to the Securities & Exchange Commission for its annual 10K filing. You do not want REITS that make mortgages, since the price of such stocks tend to tumble or worse when interest rates rise, particularly if they lend money for construction. You also don't want shares of real estate development companies. If you know what to avoid, REITs are a good way to invest in other equity real estate, since they must pass along to shareholders at least 95% of their earnings from rents and resale of buildings. Thus they pay high dividends that you can arrange with your broker to have reinvested as they are paid. You can generally expect a REIT to yield about 10% to 12% of your investment, and with any luck, the share price won't drop much as rates rise. What makes REITs different from other stocks and bonds in this respect? Dividends paid on bonds and high-yielding stocks are fixed; thus the market price of the security drops as the other rates rise. But equity REITs in a period of rising rates and mounting inflation can presumably raise the rents they charge for apartments and office space that they already own, passing most of the increased rents along to their shareholders as dividends.

Another way to invest in real estate equity is through investment partnerships. There are two problems here. First, commissions—which are built into the profit structure and are often hard to isolate—are high, running from 8% to 20%. Also, these investments are hard to resell, even though some brokerage houses are now making markets in partnership participations and may promise to buy them back. But without a public market the price at which you can sell back such trusts is set by the institution doing the buying. Neither of these things would be all that important if you intended to hold onto your real estate investment over the long haul. But real estate is being proposed here as a short-term investment to be held until interest rates stabilize at a high level.

In general neither commodities like gold nor real estate are very suitable for IRAs, since both can show big capital losses under certain market conditions.

4
Designing an IRA Portfolio for Your Needs

Now that you know which investments make the most sense for your IRA, you must go through that list and select the ones that will best fill your personal needs. As a simple measure for that, look at each of the following four criteria in terms of your own particular requirements:

1. If you are nearing retirement age, and particularly if your IRA is your only investment, you might care most about the *safety of your capital*.

2. If you have numerous other investments and won't rely on your IRA heavily during retirement, you may be willing to risk losses, even in your IRA, and go for *appreciation*. Thus the potential for big profits might be more important to you than safety.

3. If you are nearing retirement and making plans based on a specific return, or if you are counting on a specific amount of money to pay college expenses from your IRA, *volatility* becomes a big factor and you also want to make certain you get the *return* you expect. A sudden drop in the value of your IRA could cause big problems, while a windfall profit would not be necessary to further your purpose.

Here is a look at a number of investments that you could put into your IRA. Each is ranked on a scale of

0 to 3 (3 being the strongest rank) indicating how they fare in terms of a particular standard.

SAFETY OF YOUR CAPITAL

Stock Market (Blue Chip stocks)—2. If you can hold onto a conservative stockmarket investment, you stand a chance of getting back your principal, even if the price initially drops. This is also true of the following types of stockmarket mutual funds: growth, growth and income, income and balanced funds.

Stock market (Over-the-counter stocks)—1. Although profit potential is higher with these stocks than the Blue Chips, there is the danger of a single small company folding or getting into financial difficulty. There is less risk of loss, if you can hold on long enough, in an over-the-counter or aggressive growth stock mutual fund, which might be rated 2.

Treasury Bills, savings account deposits, Certificates of Deposit, and money market accounts at Federally insured banks—3. There is no risk here—all are insured or backed by the Federal government.

Long-term government bonds—2. Even though these bonds are backed by the Federal government, their resale price can drop when interest rates rise, cutting into your principal if you must sell them before maturity. The same is true of commercial bonds.

Commodities futures, stock and index options—0. These are the riskiest of all, and you not only could lose all of your principal but also many times your investment.

Straddles, spread, and hedges—2. You can turn these markets into sure things by locking in potential profits—the problem is that there is no way to make a profit if you make the bet too certain.

Commodities mutual funds and pools—1. You can lose a lot of money quickly in gold and other commodities funds, but you generally have a chance to withdraw your money before half of it is gone.

Equity real estate investments—2. While the capital value of your investment can decline, it is stabilized by the fact that your earnings will come primarily as investment income through dividends.

Fixed-rate annuities—2. Your principal is guaranteed by the insurance company writing your annuity contract and depends on the solvency of that insurer. To check the rating of an insurer, consult *Best's Insurance Reports*, which is published in Morristown, N.J. The company rates insurers in much the same way Standard & Poor's rates bonds.

APPRECIATION POTENTIAL

Some investors really want to be speculators, risking everything for a big profit. Such investors would put appreciation at the top of their list of importance.

Stock market (Blue Chip stocks)—1. Over the years profits from portfolios of Blue Chip stocks outpaced many other markets; but the potential for super profits—except in the first weeks of a big stock market turn—aren't there. Profit potential for mutual funds composed largely of such stocks would similarly rank as 1.

Stock market (Over-the-counter stocks)—2. Particularly if you invest at the end of December (since half of the annual gains usually come in January) or early in a period of low interest rates, potential for big profits is greater than with the Blue Chips. It is conceivable, for example, that you could get a 25% return on your money in three or four months; you could also lose 25% of your investment in the same time period.

Treasury Bills, savings account deposits, Certificates of Deposit, and money market accounts at Federally insured banks—0. You will get back exactly what you know you will get back right from the start—the lowest return or rate of all.

Long-term government bonds—1. Although the return or interest rate on such bonds is usually far less than low-grade corporate bonds, for example, there is still the possibility of making substantial capital gains if you lock in when interest rates are high and sell when they are rock bottom. Low-grade corporate bonds or junk bonds might rank a 2, since they combine the potential for capital gains when rates drop with a return that is usually at least 3 percentage points higher than Federally insured government issues.

Commodities futures, stock and index options—3. Here your potential profits can be astronomical—multiples of your investment—where risk is the greatest. But if you hedge or spread to reduce your risk, the profit potential can drop right down to 0.

Equity real estate investments—1. Your return comes from distribution of rents and occasional profits from sale of a building. Therefore windfall profits are unlikely.

Fixed-rate annuity—0. The rate is set at the beginning of each year and is generally tied in some fashion to the return from Treasury Bonds, hardly providing a profit bonanza.

SAFETY OF YOUR RETURN

When you are planning your future, it is often important to anticipate exactly what to expect from your investments.

Stock market—0. There are no sure things in the stock market. You can, however, often lock in a small profit by using options as a hedge, so with this strategy stocks can become a 2.

Treasury Bills, savings account deposits, Certificates of Deposit at Federally insured banks—3. That's what these short-term, low-profit securities are all about.

Money market accounts—1. You can't guarantee your return, but you can at least see a decline in rates coming. What's more you can be certain your return won't drop below, say, 5%—which would be almost tantamount to putting the economy out of business.

Long-term government bonds—3. You can absolutely lock in your return if you hold your security to maturity. If you want to lock in a return for, say, three years, you can buy bonds in the secondary market at a specific yield and you will get that return as long as you hold onto them to maturity. But if you might be forced to sell your government bonds before maturity, their ranking for safety of return would be 0. If they were bought when rates were low, their market value could plummet if rates began to rise—and that could wipe out your return.

PLANNING AN IRA AROUND YOUR FINANCIAL NEEDS

Commodities futures, stock and index options—0–3. By using straddles and hedging, profits at certain levels can be guaranteed, but the surer the return, the lower the return.

Commodities funds and pools—0. There is no way to predict how well you will fare.

Equity real estate investments—1. Barring strong market changes, you can at least come close to predicting your return from the initial prospectus or the dividend yield of the REIT stock when you purchased it. But there is also the potential for capital losses in the stock market.

Fixed-rate annuities—3. The rate is set annually by the insurer issuing the annuity, and you can be certain that is the rate you will get.

LIQUIDITY

To some investors the ability to sell an investment for immediate cash is critical. In fact, most investors would consider liquidity a desirable feature for at least a certain portion of their IRA portfolios in the case of emergency. Also, for someone intending to turn their investment portfolio into the down payment for a house or to begin withdrawing funds on a schedule for retirement, liquidity is everything.

Stock market (Blue Chip stocks)—2. You can instantly sell your exchange-listed stocks during trading hours on weekdays, unless trading in the issue has been halted for some reason. You might lose money if you have to sell under pressure, but there is little risk of losing liquidity unless the company goes bankrupt.

Stock market (Over-the-counter stocks)—1. There is often a limited float in the shares of the smallest over-the-counter stocks, which could produce delays in selling, along with the possibility of taking big losses if market makers aren't enthusiastic that day about taking on more shares. Large OTC stocks rate a 2 in liquidity, just like exchange-listed ones; and they might even be more liquid, since OTC market makers often continue to trade shares of OTC stocks despite announcements that may halt trading on the exchanges.

Treasury Bills, Certificates of Deposit—1. You ordinarily must hold onto such securities to maturity, which could be a year. If you want to sell a CD before maturity, it will usually cost you six months of earned interest. In terms of pure liquidity, these rank poorly.

Money market accounts, savings account deposits—3. You can generally withdraw your money and get every penny, including all interest you have earned, whenever the banks or brokerage houses are open.

Long-term government bonds—2. Government bonds can be quickly sold in the secondary markets, although you may have to take a capital loss.

Commodities futures, stock and index options—1. Assuming that you hold contracts in any heavily traded market, you won't have much trouble quickly closing out your position. The problem is that the nature of futures and options trading is a gamble with time (the period for which you hold the option), and the need to sell quickly for any reason would obliterate most trading strategies.

Commodity funds and pools—1–3. Commodity mutual funds that are part of a family that permits telephone switching are practically as liquid as stocks and rank a 3, although you might have to take a loss if you are forced to liquidate. Many pools rank as a 1, since most are closed-end and it can be difficult to sell your position.

Equity real estate—1–3. REIT shares can generally be sold in the stock market instantly, so these would rate a 3. Limited partnerships are more difficult, and sometimes impossible, to sell and therefore rank as a 1.

Fixed-rate annuities—1. It can be difficult and costly to withdraw your money from an insurance annuity, whether you want to use the money or move it to another institution. Surrender fees can run 10% or more, although most decrease after the first five years.

Take a close look at the four criteria—safety of capital, appreciation potential, safety of the return, and liquidity—in terms of your own specific needs. Rank them in terms of importance to you right now and in the future. If one doesn't apply—say liquidity is of no interest to you—drop it from your consideration in selecting IRA investments.

5
Strategies for Your IRA Life Cycle

It is helpful when you set up your first IRAs to decide what investment strategies you will want to use over their lifetime. Some of these decisions are easier than others. Practically everyone, as they near retirement, will want to convert their investments into liquid securities like money market accounts and Certificates of Deposit or bonds that will mature on or before each of the years the IRS requires you to make withdrawals, which begin in the year you turn seventy and one-half and continue for eleven or so years, depending on your statistical life expectancy in the eyes of the government. You must withdraw the money at least at that pace or pay serious penalties.

You can, if you want, begin withdrawing funds from your IRA in the year you turn fifty-nine and one-half. As a practical matter, you probably won't want to do that unless you are in financial need at the time or intend to take early retirement. That's because, although you won't have to pay the 10% or 20% penalty, you will have to pay income taxes on the money you withdraw. Most people fifty-nine and one-half are in a high income bracket in comparison to their potential bracket after retirement.

You may, however, intend to retire and begin withdrawing your money at age sixty-five, although seventy is more likely retirement age for people now in their thirties. Whatever age you think most likely, you will want to begin converting your investments for liquidation at least six, and possibly ten, years before the targeted retirement date. That's because you will want to liquidate stocks, stock mutual funds, bonds that you don't intend to hold until maturity, bond mutual funds, gold, and real estate holdings at the time that you can get a price at least close—and preferably equal—to what you paid. To avoid losses in your IRA, take advantage of broad market cycles, encompassing every movement of interest rates—low rates, rises, high rates, and declines to relatively low levels again. Such cycles may take a year or even five or six years to run their course. Watch market conditions closely and convert each investment into liquid or timed-maturity assets as soon as profitably possible.

A topic of far greater controversy is IRA investment strategy earlier in your life. Conventional advice is that in your early decades you might want to try venturesome investments in your IRA like real estate and stocks, converting to more conservative and safer securities in your later years. There's just one problem with this strategy—$1000 speculated and lost when you are thirty years old, with compounding, represents, say, $64,000 some thirty-six years later if you had invested at a steady 12%. On the other hand, speculating with $1000 here and $1000 there on high-risk, high-reward ventures when you are just twelve years from retirement would cost you just $4000 each time you lost all your money. It's those early dollars that really build your nest egg.

Here are some alternative life cycle strategies:

Modified life cycle. Under this strategy you would convert to liquid and timed-maturity investments in the last six to ten years, just as you would have with the speculative-to-conservative strategy. The difference is that throughout all the earlier life of your IRAs you would stick to the type of investments recommended in Chapter

3, moving from interest-rate bearing investments into some stocks, real estate, or gold when market conditions turned positive for these investments and negative for those that normally make the best use of your IRA tax shelter. A description of the market conditions that would call for such a switch are also outlined in Chapter 3.

Following this strategy, you might find yourself investing conservatively through your thirties and suddenly switching some of your IRA money into a gold mutual fund when you were fifty-six years old. But the net result would be more profits for you and less potential to show big losses that would eat up valuable IRA dollars.

The find-a-good-thing-and-stick-with-it strategy. The usual IRA investment strategy today is no strategy. Most commonly, investors buy Certificates of Deposit and roll them over into more Certificates of Deposit as they mature. With this non-strategy at least you don't endanger your principal, although there are faster ways to make your IRA grow.

Long-term bonds, even government bonds, pay more than CDs, and if you buy them in the form of zero-coupon bonds, they pay even more. You would get a better return still if you ventured into high-grade corporate bonds, especially high-grade corporate zeros. In short, if you want to use the simple approach of keeping all your IRA money in one security, shop around for an interest-bearing bond that offers an amount of risk you are willing to take and higher rates than those eighteen-month CDs.

If, on the other hand, you are happy with CDs—which take very little effort on your part—there is a strategy you can employ to get the best return over the years. If you could anticipate accurately interest rate increases and decreases, it would be easy to select the right CD maturity each time you had to roll over a mature CD into a new one. When rates were low, you would buy a CD that would mature when you expected rates to be highest and then roll your money over into a CD paying the high rates with the longest maturity that you could find. But since no one can predict with certainty when rates will hit their highs and lows, that strategy is impossible. Lacking the gift of prophecy, you will get the best overall return if you always buy the CD with the longest maturity. In general the longest CDs are usually the ones paying the most interest, but when rates are very high short-term CDs may offer the highest rates. You should buy the one with the longest maturity anyway, because in that way you will be able to lock a high return in place for, say, five years. If you opted for the higher-paying short-term CD you would risk being forced to roll your money over into a CD paying a much lower rate in three months or a year and could lose over the long run.

With the strategy outlined here there may be times you will want to withdraw all your money from your existing CDs and pay the penalty, which is usually six-months' worth of interest. (That penalty is imposed by the bank; there are no IRA penalties if you simply move your money from one CD into another.) Such a time could be to a period of sudden and very high rates. Here's an example: You buy a five-year CD paying 10% in annual interest during a period of low rates. A year later, rates are near historic highs and comparable CDs are paying 15%. Your penalty for cashing in your 10% CD would be six-months' interest or $50 for each $1000. Since you have already collected $100 interest the $50 penalty won't even cut into your $1000 principal. You then buy a new five-year CD that pays 15%. In the first year you will earn $150 interest, compared to $100 that you would have earned with the old CD. Over the remainder of the life of that CD you will earn $200 more than if you had kept the old CD.

In periods of high rates do your arithmetic and see if it makes sense to convert. Even if you don't convert, it may make sense to withdraw the interest that has accumulated in your various CDs and reinvest that at the new high rates. Technically, you can withdraw the interest you have earned without getting penalized, although your bank will probably give you a hard time. Persist.

Pick-a-rate. This strategy results in a diversified portfolio containing both super-secure and risky securities. The idea is to pick a rate—say anything from 9% to 14%, and more reasonably between 10% and 12%. You don't need any strategy to get returns of, say, 8%, since you can easily do that with bank Certificates of Deposit. And if you pick a rate higher than, say, 13%, you run the risk of accumulating a somewhat wobbly portfolio. All you do each year is select the safest type of security that offers your target rate. Over a period of decades you should build a portfolio that ranges from super-safe Treasury Bonds to shares in high-risk bond mutual funds—all paying the same rate. One advantage of this approach is that you can predict in advance how much money you will have in your IRAs at retirement. That supposes, of course, that you are able to liquidate your bond funds without losses in your six-year, pre-retirement conversion period and that you are able to hold the rest of the securities to maturity.

There are several ways to figure out what you will have to buy to get the rate you select. First, there is the chain of increasing-risk, increasing-rates that runs through the bond market. The lowest risk/rates are paid by Certificates of Deposit and Treasury Bills, and both risk and rates rise as you go up the chain of government agency securities, high-rated corporate bonds, middle-rated corporates, and poor-rated or junk corporates. *Barron's*, a weekly financial tabloid available at most large newsstands, shows rates for these various securities in a weekly table for easy comparison.

You can also get higher rates by buying the security you select in longer maturities. And purchase of anything from government securities to junk bonds in the form of zero-coupon bonds usually adds a percentage point to the yield. (See Chapter 16 for more on comparing rates paid by various bonds.) Thus, if you select 12% as your target, you might buy ten-year Treasury Bonds for one year, and for another year you might purchase shares in a mutual fund of high-risk, high-yield corporate bonds.

One other factor to keep in mind is the mix of investments that you hold outside your IRA. It goes without saying that if you decide to hold some Treasury Bonds and speculate in the stock market as well, you should put the Treasury Bonds in the IRA where they can make the best use of your IRA tax benefits, and keep the stocks on the outside.

6

Do-It-Yourself Market Timing

At any given time certain types of investments make more sense than others, which themselves might be preferable at another time under different circumstances. While libraries and computer data banks are filled with variables that affect markets, there is one measure that perhaps exceeds all others as an indicator to where your money should be. That measure is the level and direction of interest rates, and it is to investment markets what the thermometer is to disease. (To be sure, hospitals have analytical equipment ranging from brain scanners to lasers. But the first line of analysis—and the one that has remained over the years—is the thermometer.) Similarly, there are hundreds of developments filling the news that have some effect on the direction of interest rates in the various financial markets—inflation level, government spending, the Federal deficit, and so forth. But interest rates are not the only factor in making an intelligent selection of an investment market and the sort of investment that makes the most sense within that market.

In this chapter we are concerned with the general merits of specific investments rather than their particular suitability for IRA investments. If you selected certain strategies in the prior chapter—for example, if you opted for a policy of just buying long-term Treasury Bonds and holding them to maturity—it may be unnecessary or even confusing for you to attempt to track market trends in the fashion suggested by this chapter. But for an investor who expects to use a more complex strategy, such as the modified life cycle, for his IRA and who also intends to do some investing outside his IRA, the suggestions in this chapter for detecting and acting on market turns should prove invaluable.

For a small investor it is enough to check interest rates once a week or even once a month. For the purpose of our rundown we're using rates for the ninety-day Treasury Bill which can be found daily in most newspapers. By charting the rate of ninety-day Treasury Bills once each month the small investor at least has a chance to get into each new market soon after the latest market trends have gotten underway.

The rundown that follows shows where you should move your investment dollars when Treasury Bill rates are high, when they turn and begin to fall, when they are low, and when they begin to climb. Here two questions emerge: How low is low? As an arbitrary rule use 7.5% and lower. How high is high? Use figure levels over 9.5%.

Now here's your market cycle list:

When rates are high. This is the time to lock into *long-term bonds*—for twenty years or longer, if possible. And it is a particularly good time to lock into zero-coupon bonds for your IRA, since rates for zeros are usually a bit higher than comparable coupon-paying bonds. Don't be enticed into buying shorter bonds or put your money into money market funds where rates may be even higher than for the long bonds in periods of very high interest. Remember, the high rates will be gone by the time your investment matures, and you'll be left holding the bag. In fact, when short-term rates exceed long-term rates it is a sure sign that rates are peaking and the best time of all to lock into long-term bonds.

As for *stocks*, all the financial planner chatter about stocks being an inflation hedge is misleading. When interest rates are high and steady, stock prices—as measured by the usual indexes—tend to be low and steady. If you want to buy equities, look for stocks with big dividends. Most stock quote tables give not only the size of the dividend for each stock but its yield based on each day's closing price for the stock. If you buy high-yielding stocks, particularly utilities, when rates are high you will have the benefit of the dividend plus some hope of capital gains as interest rates fall and stock prices begin to rise. So hold onto them. Their behavior is similar to that of long-term bonds, which also rise in market price as interest rates fall.

Similarly, *mutual funds* composed of high-yielding stocks or income funds that combine high-yielding stocks and bonds make a good investment when rates are high.

Real estate investments may offer opportunities in high-rate periods. In an effort to stay competitive during such periods, they often include so-called equity kickers for mortgage lenders to attract investors.

When interest rates start to fall. This is when big profits can be made in the stock market and the bond market. *Bond Prices* begin to rise as interest rates fall, and you can watch the market value of your bonds go up, up, up all the way down the interest-rate slide. At that point you can sell them if you want—reaping big profits—or you can continue collecting big returns while around you rates are bottoming. *Bond mutual funds* work almost exactly the same as the actual bonds. If you buy fund shares at a particular price, you lock in your yield, and as the prices of shares rise and interest rates fall, the value of your shares rises.

This is also definitely the time to get into the *stock market*, as the big market turns take place midstream in big rate drops. You can either buy stocks early and wait for the turnaround, or you can keep your eyes open and pounce when the turn comes. Typically certain stocks move first in a turnaround. So you should start with Blue Chips—like the thirty stocks that make up the Dow Jones Industrial Average (see Chapter 27)—and interest-sensitive stocks like those of banks or insurance companies or stocks of the brokerage houses. Brokerage shares respond immediately to any turn and quickly compound faster than any others.

Stock mutual funds that buy their stocks to reflect one of the market indexes (index funds) or traditional funds that buy Blue Chip stocks make the most sense in a turnaround. You would do better to buy the actual stocks, perhaps through a discount broker, and save the mutual fund management fee since only moderate risk is involved.

If you're a speculator, the turnarounds make big opportunities for profit in the *options* market. But here you have the added problem of calling the exact moment of the turn, which means options on the stocks and indexes are still a risk. The biggest potential bonanza comes from buying options on the stock of a brokerage house like Merrill Lynch just as the market begins its turn.

This is a market for *shorting*—selling in expectation of a price downturn. *Commodities*—specifically the agricultural ones and gold and other metals—are good prospects for selling, as their prices tend to tumble with interest rates. As for *financial futures*, this is a time to buy, since their prices rise when rates fall. And it is a good time to sell off any *tangibles*—art, antiques, or collectibles—and take the gains.

When interest rates are low. As long as you get out when short-term rates rise to the level of your long-term yield, you can beat the market by parking in a high-yield, high-risk *bond fund*. Ideally you should invest through a mutual fund family that will permit you to phone your orders to them to instantly switch your money into a money market fund when rates start to rise. This is an instance where investment in a bond mutual fund makes much more sense than buying the actual high-risk bond. That's because the mutual fund blunts the potential risk of failure of any one such bond.

A good place to have your money in low-interest periods is the *stock market*. Over-the-counter and other possibly undiscovered stocks are worth considering, since they tend to move upward in price late in the market cycle. *Stock mutual funds* that concentrate on growth stocks are your best bet when interest rates are low and flat. But be sure to get out of the stock market and stock mutual funds quickly when rates turn upward.

Commodities don't make a particularly good investment when interest rates are flat—whether they are high or low—since commodities profits come from movement up or down.

When interest rates start to rise. *Money market funds* are good when interest rates begin to rise, even if the money market is still paying low interest. That's because rising rates set investors off in a scramble to protect their capital, or actual investment.

Bond and stock market prices tumble as rates rise, and if you don't switch rapidly from stocks into the money market, you could suffer losses. This is a good time, however, to speculate in the *options* markets—short selling stocks, bonds and indexes (see Chapter 31). Even here, though, there are no sure things, since rising rates have been known to turn into a tumble midstream, and if you get caught in options, you could lose your shirt.

Similarly, *commodities* are hot when rates start to rise— particularly the agricultural ones and gold and precious metals. That's because rising rates bring renewed prospects of inflation which is reflected in the prices of things like gold, petroleum, and wheat.

This is also a good time to buy *tangibles*—art, antiques, and collectibles—which also make good hedges against inflation and tend to peak in price when interest rates are the highest. When rates are low, prices of tangibles tend to be low as well. But remember, you can't put tangibles in your IRA.

7
New Tax Laws and Your Investments

Major tax reform is coming by 1987, and it will change the way you spend, borrow and invest. The coming tax reform has been called a deterrent to investment by its critics, who contend its major effect will be to encourage you to spend more money, and invest less.

A close reading of the bill that passed the House of Representatives, and at this writing awaits action by the Senate, suggests the biggest result will be a cutback in borrowing, since interest payments—other than those on your home mortgage—will no longer be deductible. As for your home, you will still be able to write off the interest on your primary residence for tax purposes. And under reform you would still be able to roll over gains on the sale of your primary residence if you buy a new home within two years after the sale. Homeowners who are fifty-five years old or older would still be able to exclude permanently from taxable income or capital gains taxes the first $125,000 of inflation-adjusted gain on their principal residence.

Reform, if it becomes law in its current form, will create some changes in the way you invest and will close some loopholes that in the past helped individuals build tax-free income to finance such expenditures as college educations for their children. While Clifford Trusts and other vehicles to put investments in the name of your children to cut or eliminate taxes are headed toward the trash heap, alternative strategies are included in this book.

PLANNING AN IRA AROUND YOUR FINANCIAL NEEDS

(See the introduction to this section; Chapter 21, and Part IV for tax-paring ways to save for college educations and home down payments under coming reform.)

Perhaps the biggest knock to investing for the average individual is a plan to shrink the total amount a person can invest, tax-free, in IRAs, Keoghs and sheltered pension plans. Reform would put an annual umbrella of $7000 or $8000 on such investments by an individual. Currently one person could, theoretically, have an IRA, Keogh Plan for part-time earnings and 401-k Plan through his full-time employer, putting more than $62,000 into these shelters in a single year (see Chapter 10).

In other ways, however, the new tax law promises to make investing more profitable for you. For a married couple with one non-working spouse the annual IRA limit would be expanded to $4000 from the current $2250 level. And lower basic income tax rates will permit more of the interest you earn to remain in your pocket or bank account. It is expected that the maximum tax rate will drop to 35%–38% from the current 50% level. That should encourage investment in interest-bearing securities, where investment income is taxed at the same rate as ordinary income. Reduced taxes will also remove some of the incentive to hold onto investments until they qualify for long-term capital gains taxes. It is likely that long-term capital gains will continue to be taxed at a maximum of around 20%, the current level; while short-term capital gains, which are taxed at the same level as income, will be taxed at the 35%–38% level, down from a maximum of 50%.

None of this, of course, will affect your IRA, although it will make investing outside your IRA more profitable. It will also make in-and-out trading, where a speculator rapidly buys and sells stocks or other securities for a quick profit, more feasible since the short-term capital gains tax will drop.

There is good news for investors who invest in tax-free

municipal bonds to reduce their tax bill. Municipals will remain tax free, although some non-municipals that formerly enjoyed tax protection will no longer be tax-free. If you hold industrial development bonds or other similar tax-free non-municipals, don't worry. Your existing tax-exempt bonds will no doubt be protected by a grandfather clause and continue tax-exempt until they mature.

PART II

Setting Up Your Investment Accounts

ONCE you decide on your investment strategy, you are ready to open your investment accounts. This isn't as simple as it seems, and you may end up opening more than one account, even if all you intend to do this year is put $1000 into your IRA.

For many small investors a good place to start is with an account at one of the mutual fund management companies running a telephone switching service among an assortment of no-load mutual funds (see Chapter 11). These give you many of the services you will want along with a variety of options, including funds that invest in everything from the money market to gold.

But there are some things you can't do through most

mutual fund management companies. For example, you can't buy zero-coupon bonds, get into real estate or commodities investment plans, buy actual stocks, or buy bonds that you can hold to maturity. You can do all these things through big full-service brokerage houses, but most don't have no-load (no front-end sales fee) funds with telephone switching privileges. What's more, some investors prefer the personal services of investment boutiques or little regional brokerage firms, although these don't have many of the high-technology frills or services.

Another possibility is an account with a discount broker, particularly one associated with a big bank—like Chase Manhattan's Rose & Co. or Charles Schwab, which is a unit of the Bank of America. And for buying stocks and bonds there are even cheaper discount brokers (see Chapter 14). You an do almost aanything imaginable through a Schwab account, from telephone switching among no-load mutual funds (although each switch involves a brokerage commission that wouldn't be charged if you switched directly through a no-load mutual fund management company) to purchase of zero-coupon bonds. But even the big multiservice discount brokers don't offer investment advice, and for many small investors that triggers feelings of insecurity.

If you have enough money to invest, you may want to set up your IRAs through the trust department of a good bank. Such an account—particularly for a self-administered IRA—offers a wide variety of investment options, but it can be expensive. Or you may want to seek out an insurance company to consider a retirement annuity. To make all these options more confusing, there are crossovers in the services they offer. Some insurers also act as mutual fund managers for no-load families. And some mutual fund managers are discount stockbrokers.

Let's look at the IRA life cycle strategies outlined in Chapter 5 for an idea of what kinds of accounts are best for each strategy, and what accounts may be appropriate for investments make outside your IRA.

Find-a-good-thing-and-stick-with-it. If the good thing you find is a CD, shop around for rates and set up an IRA with the Federally insured bank that makes the best offer. (Stay away from state-insured banks, even though they sometimes offer substantially better rates. Some problems have already occurred with such banks.)

You can also buy Treasury Bills, Notes, and Bonds through most banks. One problem is that these only come in $5000 or $10,000 denominations. So if your good thing is a Treasury security, you may have to open an account with a full-service or discount stockbroker who offers Treasury-backed zero-coupon bonds, which come in $1000 shares.

You may also want a stockbroker if you decide to put your money into high-quality corporate bonds. An alternative is to open an account with a no-load mutual fund family that offers funds composed of Treasuries, Ginnie Maes, or whatever you select. The problem here is that you can't hold your securities to maturity, since mutual funds keep reinvesting and the fund shares never mature. As a result, you may have to hold your fund shares for years while you wait for the price to come back to what you paid so you can convert.

If you select CDs as your good thing, you might also want to shop around and check rates that insurance companies are paying on IRA annuities, which are similar to CDs in that they can pay a fixed rate. And you should check with your credit union, if you have one, since credit unions offer a security similar to a CD that may pay slightly better rates. Some stockbrokers also offer CDs, but you probably won't want to buy them, since you will have to pay trading commissions that aren't imposed when you buy CDs directly from a bank.

Even if you use the one-good-thing strategy, you should

shop around annually for rates and probably will end up with IRAs at several different institutions.

Pick-a-Rate. With this strategy you will need to look at the same institutions as the one-good-thing investor. The difference is that you will probably want to set up a variety of accounts with brokers, mutual funds and banks right away, since from one year to the next you will want to be able to select from the full range of interest-bearing investments suited for IRAs.

A telephone switching account with a mutual fund management company might be useful. These families offer money market funds and funds made up of securities like Ginnie Maes, which you might not be able to buy directly because they come in $10,000 minimum size units. You generally pay less commission when you buy Ginnie Mae no-load mutual fund shares rather than Ginnie Mae unit trusts from stockbrokers. You can hold the unit trust shares to maturity, however.

The problem with switching families for the pick-a-rate strategy is that there is no guarantee that you will get back all your principal, which defeats the point of locking in a specific rate.

Modified life cycle. With this strategy you will need both brokerage and switching-family accounts as outlined for the pick-a-rate strategy. You will also want to make sure that the mutual fund family you select for fund switching has a gold fund and a high-yield high-risk junk bond fund with a reasonably good track record.

In short, you must sit down and figure out the accounts you will need and then shop around. Ask lots of questions about rates, services, variety of investments available, minimums and restrictions on switching from investment to investment. We'll take a closer look in the following chapters.

8

Picking Your IRA Administrator

One of the most important investment decisions you will ever make is your choice of where you open your IRA. You are not just picking the institution that will act as custodian or trustee for your Individual Retirement Account money. You are also predetermining who will make decisions about investing that money, how much risk you will take with your retirement dollars, and how much you will ultimately have in your retirement account.

Below are several questions you should consider to help you make the right selection:

How much time and attention, realistically, are you willing and able to give to your investment account? If you are willing at least once a week to read an investment column, check prices and rates of your various investments, and devote an hour or two to your investment strategy, you should at least consider a self-administered IRA and choose the type of trustee that will permit you to do that. But if you know you will let your accounts slide for months, you will do better to set up a simple trustee-run IRA. Commercial banks, savings and loan companies, savings banks, and insurance companies all offer trustee-run accounts, which you may see advertised in their windows. Your employer or credit union may also be equipped to set up an IRA for you—if so, it probably would be trustee-run.

One type of IRA account that would be relatively effort-free is a Certificate of Deposit that can be automatically rolled over or renewed each time it expires. Before each expiration date you will be contacted by the trustee to approve renewal, which can be done by mail. Other than that, your trustee-run IRA takes no tending.

Equally effort-free are IRA annuity accounts with an insurance company. It is possible to open an IRA annuity account that offers you a pre-set rate of return and contribute to it over the years any amount of money within the legal limits at any pace you wish. In the end you can take your money as a lump sum or as pre-set annuity payments of a monthly sum for life.

You should call a number of institutions and compare potential annual yield of the IRA investments they offer. Yield represents the compounding interest in an account. As a result the yield on an investment is slightly higher than its interest rate. So don't compare yield on one investment to the interest rate of another investment—that's comparing apples to oranges.

In addition to yield, be sure you ask about entry, maintenance, and withdrawal charges levied on investments, since they vary widely from one institution to another. Also compare services offered by the various institutions. Some, for example, provide automatic deductions from your bank account to your IRA on a monthly basis or will arrange for payroll deduction.

How much money do you have to invest? Many securities brokers feel it makes little sense to open self-administered IRA accounts with brokerage houses before you have, say, $8000 in your IRAs. That's partly because trading fees must come directly from the tax-sheltered dollars in your IRA, and when you are moving small amounts of money around, minimum commissions

SETTING UP YOUR INVESTMENT ACCOUNTS

(usually $35 per trade) can rapidly eat up your compounding dollars. In addition, entry, administrative, and withdrawal fees for self-run IRA plans with brokers and banks tend to be higher than for trustee-run plans.

Today the average accumulated IRA is about $3,500, although some individuals and families have accumulated substantially more than that, sometimes by terminating pension plans and rolling over the funds—which may amount to $25,000 and more—into their IRA.

If you would like to run your own IRA but have less than $8000, you should consider opening an IRA with one of the mutual fund families that permit telephone switching from fund to fund.

Most provide at least five different types of mutual funds: conservative and higher-risk stock market funds, various types of government and commercial bond funds, and a money market fund. Quite a few also offer some more venturesome funds, including gold funds, foreign funds and Ginnie Mae funds.

Where families offer no-load funds—which don't have front-end fees—you switch investments without having to pay the trading fees a stockbroker would charge (see Chapter 11).

How good is your basic knowledge of investment? If you have little background in investment, the research and advisory services of full-service brokerage houses are a must. If, however, you are well grounded in investment, you should consider setting up your IRA with a discount broker, where trading fees are substantially lower than full-service brokers. Some discount brokers are also promoting IRA plans that involve no entry, maintenance, or termination fees.

Picking the Administrator
ADMINISTRATORS: OFFERINGS AND CHARGES

Institution	Cost and fees	Trading charges	Common investment	Common services	Risk
Savings & loans/ savings banks (trustee-run)	Usually none; a few charge small ($10) entry fees—watch for future in-account administration fees; big withdrawal penalties	None	Fixed-rate CDs (six-month to five year maturities); savings accts (variable rate)	Automatic rollover of CDs; automatic monthly savings acct deductions	Most Federally insured; beware state-insured banks
Commercial banks (trustee-run)	Usually none	None	Fixed-rate CD's (six-month to five years); floating-rate money market accts	Rates fixed for term of CD; automatic rollover; monthly deductions	Federally insured

(self-run)	Entry fee; annual admin. fee (can be $120 a year); separate billing	Pass-through commissions	Stocks; mutual funds; bonds; money market accts; possibly real estate and commodity funds (through offering brokers)	Some permit you to do the trading; automatic withdrawals from your bank accts	Some privately insured
Securities brokerage houses	Varies; can cost $10–$50 to open acct; sometimes withdrawal charges; big up-front fee (20% or more) with some syndicated funds like real estate	Fees for buying & selling—stocks run about $35 per buy & sell for $1000 of a $10 stock; most have $30–$35 per trade minimums	Stocks, bonds, mutual funds, zero coupons, money market accts; some also offer bank CDs, stock options, real estate and commodities funds (their own)	Telephone 800-numbers for switching investments; access to research and expert advice	Most SIPC and/or privately insured; risk of loss or low return varies by investment

Institution	Costs and fees	Trading charges	Common investment	Common services	Risk
Securities discount brokers (self-run)	Varies; a few promise no entry, administrative, or withdrawal fees	Fees for buying and selling stocks run 25% to 65% below full-service brokers; but $35 minimums per trade can wipe out the difference	Stocks, bonds, mutual funds; Schwab about to offer bank CDs; a few offer options (no syndicated real estate or commodities)	Telephone numbers (Some 800-numbers) for switching investments; some give telephone quotes, but no research or expert advice	SIPC and privately insured (Some don't carry private insurance for losses over $100,000)

| Mutual fund families (self-run) | Varies; can run $5–30 to open acct; annual maintenance fees of $20–$150 billed outside IRA; termination fees | No charge among no-load funds; run $5 per switch with low-load and some load; can run 8¼% of investment to buy some load funds | Most families have at least five choices including low- and high-risk stock funds, bond funds and a money market fund; some have gold funds, energy funds, Ginnie Mae funds, NY tax-exempt etc. | Telephone switching with 800-number; automatic dividend reinvestment plans for bond funds; some plans offer monthly bank acct deductions | Some privately insured |

Institution	Costs and fees	Trading charges	Common investment	Common services	Risk
Insurance companies (trustee-run Individual Retirement Annuity Accts)	Usually no entry fee but heavy withdrawal fee before five years; maintenance fees (annual) can run over $100—watch that such fees aren't charged directly to variable annuities	None	Fixed or variable rate annuities; choice of investment type on some variable ones	Guaranteed rate of return on fixed annuity; may be rolled over into fixed-payment retirement annuity at maturity or select this option at outset. (Payout from non-insurer IRAs qualify for this option from insurers.)	Insured by industry funds and some private coverage
(Self-run)	See information on mutual fund families, above				

Your employer (Trustee-run; group IRA's)	Usually none	Single option chosen by employer	Payroll deduction	Varies
Credit union (trustee-run)	Usually none	Certificates similar to bank CDs	Deduction	Federally insured

9
Running Your Own IRA

Technically, you can put all sorts of things in an IRA. Soy bean oil futures, physical real estate, hot little over-the-counter stocks, and even fancy options straddles are all okay according to the Internal Revenue Service. That is, you can put these things in your IRA if you set up a self-directed one. The first trick is figuring out whether they make any sense as part of your retirement investment strategy. And the second trick is finding a trustee or custodian who will let you do whatever it is that you decide you want to do.

You can buy everything from gold funds, to long-term bond funds, including Ginnie Mae (Government National Mortgage Association) funds and even some options funds through most self-directed IRAs set up with managers of large mutual fund families, full-service brokerage houses, big discount brokers that handle mutual fund shares, and the trust departments of many banks. Generally such institutions will permit you to switch out of these funds with a phone call and redirect your money into a money market fund or account when market conditions change.

These self-directed IRAs are quite different from the garden variety of IRA you see advertised in bank windows, which generally offers you a selection of Certificates of Deposit. But a self-directed IRA is just as easy to open. All you do is ask for literature and an application, fill it out, and send the money. You can often do it by mail.

What can you buy through your self-directed IRA? At one time, virtually anything. IRAs came into existence in 1974 as part of the government's overhaul of its pension laws. At that time you heard little about them since only people who did not work for an employer with a pension plan were eligible for IRAs. They were, however, the darlings of the accounting profession, which set them up for many of their clients. At the time anything from gold bars to limited-edition collector's plates to antiques was eligible for IRAs, as long as it was kept in a bank vault. Unfortunately, scammers began pitching get-rich schemes to the accountants and their clients. Ads typically hawked returns of 60% and more on diamonds or gold, frequently backed by nothing at all.

When Congress opened up IRAs to any salaried worker in 1981, it outlawed certain IRA investments—most notably, art works, rugs, antiques, metals including silver and gold bullion, coins, stamps, gems including diamonds and emeralds, alcoholic beverages such as vintage port or wine, and certain other tangible personal property. You also may not buy any life insurance (although various forms of non-insurance annuities are available for IRAs from life insurance companies) and you can't pledge the money in your IRA account as security against a loan. Nor can you do any self-dealing, such as creating for yourself an investment in a second mortgage on your own home—although a few bank trust departments, such as the Bank of San Diego (Calif.) will let you buy trust deeds, which are pieces of someone else's second mortgage.

For your self-directed IRA, you can buy non-leveraged real estate limited partnerships from any securities house that forms them. If you do, look for non-leveraged or all-equity ones that are being structured specifically for

IRAs and tax-protected accounts. They generally yield more than 10% a year for a tax-protected account. Ordinary leveraged real estate partnerships promise to yield substantially more, based primarily on their ability to borrow or leverage their real estate purchases. This is useless to you in an IRA and pending a ruling by the IRS could even cause tax problems.

All-cash partnerships are growing in popularity for IRAs. In 1985 Merrill Lynch sold its own customers, in $1000 chunks, a $500 million all-cash real estate limited partnership in which 77% of the investors bought shares for their IRA or Keogh (Keogh is a tax-sheltered retirement plan for self-employed people). A year earlier when Merrill had offered a big low-leveraged real estate partnership only 21% of the investment represented IRA/Keogh plans.

One problem in shopping for real estate partnerships is that you can only buy them from the firm that creates them, and then only when the firm is in the process of setting up a new one. You can't trade in and out of these funds in the normal manner. You can't, for example, buy participations in the Merrill Lynch real estate partnership from Charles Schwab & Co. (a discount broker affiliated with Bank of America). It is possible, however, to set up IRA accounts with several brokerage houses and banks, providing of course, that your total annual investment doesn't exceed the legal limit of $2000 for an individual.

You can open a self-directed IRA account and buy most other things from Schwab and other large full-service discount brokers. For example, as soon as you open your Schwab IRA account you can buy stocks from the exchanges or over-the-counter market, corporate bonds, zero-coupon bonds, government securities, or shares of more than 200 no-load and low-load mutual funds that include everything from gold funds to funds that specialize in oil stocks. After subjecting you to a

SETTING UP YOUR INVESTMENT ACCOUNTS

little scrutiny and filling out of some more forms, most large brokers will even let you dabble in options. Most commonly you are allowed to write covered-call options against stocks in your portfolio. That means you can collect premiums for selling the calls—which can supplement your return in a bad or flat market—while running the risk that the stock could be called away at a price lower than you would get in the marketplace. Some brokerage houses—including Prudential/Bache Securities—offer even more sophisticated options strategies in IRA accounts of proved and knowledgeable investors.

Perhaps the highest potential for both profits and losses comes in the area of commodities futures. Technically there is nothing in IRS regulations that prohibits you from buying commodities futures contracts on pork bellies or anything else. As a practical matter such trading could force you to overinvest, borrow, commingle funds, or lose more than your IRA investment, all of which are prohibited, unwise, and might result in tax penalities. And you probably can't find a legitimate trustee who will let you dabble in futures contracts in your IRA.

Commodities mutual funds are another matter. Such funds generally spread their investments over 20 or more kinds of commodities futures contracts ranging from soy bean oil futures to Treasury Bills. That lessens both the great risk and the chance of enormous reward. Your biggest risk is that you will lose all your money. And although you can lose money quite quickly in a commodities fund, most stop trading if more than 50% of the capital is lost and permit you to get out if you want. In years when commodities prices move strongly up or down, profits in such a fund can be substantial. A study of seventeen funds by the *Managed Account Reports* newsletter showed the average rate of return after fees and commissions in 1980 was 40.8%. More recently, however, commodities markets have been directionless and the same funds averaged a 9.8% loss in 1983. Obviously you wouldn't want to risk everything in your IRA accounts on such an investment (see Chapter 33).

Most commodities funds don't sell shares for less than $5000, but more than a dozen public funds have been set up to accommodate IRA investors, and some of the firms setting these up are IRA trustees. Thomson McKinnon Securities, for example, has completed a large commodities futures fund that offered $1000 shares for IRAs; it plans to set up more such funds in the future. You could set up an IRA with Thomson McKinnon to buy shares of the fund, or you could acquire the shares through an IRA at a bank trust department that will let you do that. Many of the biggest securities houses, however, won't let you buy commodities for your IRA in any form.

Many brokerage houses will permit you to transfer IRA investments in such funds or pools into your IRA account with their company. But few, if any, sell them to their own customers. One reason is that most retail brokerage houses don't set up commodities funds, which are closed-ended like Merrill's real estate partnerships. You have to buy them from their own managers, who seldom are IRA custodians. For the same reason, most bank trust departments can't channel your IRA investment into commodities funds. But if you are still hellbent on putting commodities fund shares in your IRA, you may choose to open a self-directed account with the trust department of the Bank of San Diego or the Enterprise Bank in Washington, D.C., or one of the few other banks with trust departments that permit you to go out and acquire your own IRA investments and turn the documentation and custody over to them.

Currently, self-directed IRAs account for less than one-fourth of the nation's IRA accounts, but this is the fastest-growing kind of IRA.

As your IRA accounts get larger, it makes increasing

SETTING UP YOUR INVESTMENT ACCOUNTS

sense to learn about investments and attempt to direct at least some of your own. But watch out. When lots of unschooled investors suddenly have large amounts to invest, scammers come out of the woodwork. Beware of claims that sound too good to be true (they probably are) and stick to established institutions.

10

Other Tax Shelter for Retirement

With IRAs being hawked as such a godsend throughout the land, it's regarded as almost un-American not to set one up each year, even if all you can cough up is $500.

The fact is that not everyone can save taxes by setting up an IRA, and not everyone should have one. On the other hand, some people should have not only IRAs but also Keogh plans, SEP accounts and 401-k plans to shelter a part of their income from taxes. You may be eligible for such plans and not even know it.

Keogh plans were named for the Congressman who proposed the original legislation; 401-ks, for the 1978 tax code amendment that created them, and SEPs are the nickname for Simplified Employee Pension plans, which were created in 1978 as a corporate variety of the IRA. IRAs and SEPs were later broadened with the Economic Recovery Tax Act of 1981. All these plans permit you to take a portion of today's income and shelter it from taxes until you retire and begin withdrawing your savings and investment income in annual lumps. The idea is that you save in two ways: First, the money you put into one of these accounts reduces your taxable income today. Second, you don't pay taxes on income earned from interest and capital gains until you begin withdrawals, permitting your invested money to mount up much faster than if your profits were taxed immediately.

SETTING UP YOUR INVESTMENT ACCOUNTS

None of these plans, including IRAs, make much sense if you are relatively young with a low income in a low tax bracket, or if for any other reason you might need to withdraw your money along the way. With all but 401-k plans you can't even use any of the funds as collateral to borrow money against your account, and even that may well change under the new tax laws.

In short, there are people who won't benefit today from any of these tax-sheltered retirement plans. There are other people who should be putting money in two or even three of these government-sanctioned retirement savings accounts.

Individual Retirement Accounts (IRAs) are the best known of the four kinds of tax-sheltered retirement accounts. The size limitations of Keoghs, SEPs, and 401-k plans are all substantially higher than for IRAs, permitting you to sock away even more tax-free investment money—that is, if any of these plans are offered by your employer or if you are self-employed or have a source of income separate from your job. But under the new tax laws you won't be able to put more than $7000–$8000 a year into the combination of all your sheltered retirement vehicles, including IRAs.

All permit basically the same kind of investments as IRAs and operate under similar rules that permit withdrawal after age fifty-nine and one-half and require some withdrawal after seventy and one-half. In a 401-k it's always your company's management that selects the investment; with Keoghs, SEPs, and IRAs you have the opportunity to take control, unless the account has been set up for you by an employer.

But to get a 401-k account you must work for a corporation that offers this as one of their benefits. Since more than half of the nation's largest companys now have 401-ks, you should consult your personnel office or even suggest to management that your company consider providing this type of account to employees. Where 401-ks are offered, the company usually contributes to your account at the same time you contribute, matching 25% to 100% of your contributions in company stock or other assets. Your limit is substantially higher than the $2000 limit on IRAs for individuals. You can have an IRA and participate in a 401-k plan too. In fact, you can even have a Keogh on the side.

Your best bet in the past if you had all these alternatives was to fully fund your 401-k before moving on to put money in your IRA or a Keogh. In the 401-k you benefit from your employer's contributions, which an also boost a SEP or Keogh if you are an employee. But beyond that, your 401-k contributions never show up on your W-2 form, putting you into a lower tax bracket. And, in some cases, your 401-k account qualifies for favorable ten-year income averaging when you begin to take distribution—although that too may change under the new tax law. IRA funds, on the other hand, count as part of your regular income and all you may use is the less-favorable five-year income averaging.

While IRAs and 401-k plans apply to savings from your salary from your regular job, two other plans are useful for outside part-time earnings or as substitute retirement plans for the self-employed and employees of law firms, doctors, and other small or unincorporated businesses. Technically, you could have an IRA and, through your employer, a 401-k, along with a Keogh plan or SEP plan for your part-time earnings.

Consulting fees and payments for acting on a board of directors, freelance writing, and driving a cab at night all offer opportunities to shelter income through Keoghs. You are permitted to shelter up to your allowable limit or 20% of eligible income with a Keogh and 15% with an SEP.

A major difference of the Keogh from other plans is the red tape involved. Realistically, you need a lawyer or accountant to open a Keogh and deal with the paperwork. You can open a SEP (Simplified Employee Pension Plan) with a half-page tax form (5305-SEP)—as easily as you set up your IRA. And most institutions that will act as trustee for your IRA also will assist you in setting up a SEP, even if your SEP is extended to several employees. Keoghs and SEPs require you to set up similar plans for your employees if you have any. And with either one you can have a separate IRA with its own $2000 annual limit—as long as your total shelter doesn't exceed the total allowable limit.

RETIREMENT PROGRAMS

Tax-sheltered account	Type of income eligible	Maximum* investment	Allowable investments	Other shelters allowed	Trustee or custodian
IRA	Salary income, including fees and commissions NOT ELIGIBLE: Income from investments; Social Security etc.	$2000 for salaried individual; $2250 for married couple with non-salaried spouse; up to 100% of salary eligible*	Anything except collectibles or life insurance	SEP; Keogh; 401-k; company pension	Commercial bank; savings bank; securities house; insurance company
Group IRA	Same as IRA but with payroll deduction	Same as IRA	Same as IRA (employer's choice)	Same as IRA	Same as IRA (employer's choice)

SEP (assuming you set up SEP for yourself)	Pre-tax income from incorporated or unincorporated business; can be freelance income separate from regular job; consulting fees, etc.	Less than $30,000 or 15% of income, whichever is less*	Same as IRA	IRA, 401-k	Same as IRA (employee may change trustee or investment)
Keogh (Assuming you set up Keogh for yourself)	Pre-tax income from unincorporated business only; can be freelance income separate from regular job, consulting fees, etc.	Less than $30,000 or 20% of income, whichever is less*	Same as IRA but life insurance okay	IRA; 401-k	Same as IRA but may be own trustee; lawyer needed

Tax-sheltered account	Type of income eligible	Maximum* investment	Allowable investments	Other shelters allowed	Trustee or custodian
401-k	Pre-salary income; must be set up by employer who also contributes to your account	Less than $30,000 or 25% of salary, whichever is less*	Same as IRA, employer's choice	All	Same as IRA, employer's choice

Tax-sheltered account rules	Who makes investment decisions?	Filing requirements/ deadlines	Method of payout	Borrowing provisions
IRA	Trustee or you	April 15 of following year; fill simple application; no special form at tax time	Rolled over into annuity or must begin withdrawing funds after age 70½, taxed as ordinary income, no 10-year income averaging	Cannot secure a loan with an IRA, nor borrow money for over 60 days.
Group IRA	Your employer	Same as IRA	Same as IRA	Same as IRA
SEP	You, whether employee or employer	April 15 of following year	Same as IRA	Same as IRA

Tax-sheltered account rules	Who makes investment decisions?	Filing requirements/ deadlines	Method of payout	Borrowing provisions
Keogh	You or independent trustee or institution of deposit	Dec. 31 of same year	Same as IRA but can 10-year income average	Same as IRA; loans no longer allowed
401-k	Your employer	Dec. 31 of same year	Same as IRA but can 10-year income average	Some borrowing allowed under a formula

*Under new tax laws an umbrella of $7000–$8000 will be placed over your total in all of these tax shelter programs.

11

Telephone Switching and Fund Families

One relatively new form of investment may well be the best way for do-it-yourself IRA investors to get started, even with investments of $1000 or less. It is called telephone switching.

You can make investment decisions yourself, deciding when to move your money from one fund to another, or you can make decisions based on information supplied by market timers—technicians that follow a number of market indicators and attempt to predict when market conditions are changing.

Telephone switching, quite simply, is a procedure by which you can move all or part of your invested money from one mutual fund to another—from a fund specializing in high-growth stocks to one invested in gold shares, for example—with a toll-free telephone call to a company that manages a number of specialized mutual funds. Today more than twenty mutual fund management companies are set up to let you do this through five or more no-load or low-load (less than $5) mutual funds that invest in everything from government-insured mortgages to the money markets to international stocks.

With no-load funds, or ones without front-end charges, there is usually no fee for switching. Some funds, however, limit the number of times in a year you can switch funds. Fidelity, for example, limits annual switches to four.

Basically, switching is a kind of do-it-yourself portfolio management that can be used by even relatively unsophisticated investors. The idea is that you move your money around rather than plunking it down in one place such as a money market fund or General Motors stock and leaving it there. "Over the long term it is simply better to switch than to buy and hold," says Nancy Wyatt of the Switch Fund Advisory Service, one of the big market timing services.

On average, over the five years through 1984, if you had followed the exact advice of one of the few large market-timing services that have been around that long (today there are more than two dozen and their individual advice in most markets varies), you would have had an annual return of more than 20% on your investment—at least this is what most of the services claim. And while some critics charge that the market timers are stacking the deck, there is no question that by following advice of a good timer and switching your money from fund to fund accordingly, you can beat the performance of most single investments. There are simply times it doesn't make sense to stay parked in stocks, bonds, or money market funds.

In the case of no-load funds (no up-front fee to get in), there is usually no charge for switching from fund to fund and the transfer is immediate. No-load switching has become so popular many fund managers are permitting switching among load funds (up-front fees to get in are usually around 8% of your investment) with just a token switching fee of $5 or so. You must check fees carefully, however, before you open your account.

Today you have a wide selection of possible funds, and you should study those offered by several mutual fund families before you make your selection. If you plan to stay parked in a mutual fund for a long time, it makes

SETTING UP YOUR INVESTMENT ACCOUNTS

little difference if you choose a no-load fund or one with a front-end load. But for switching, no-load or low-load funds are essential. Funds that have a front-end load charge you money to sign up; no-load funds do not. You generally pay a lower annual management fee in load funds (where you paid the sales charges up front) than in no-load funds—so the total costs come out relatively the same unless you intend to do regular switching.

To make a selection get the names of management companies by looking in the *Wall Street Journal* or *Barron's* under the listing for quotations for mutual funds. Look for families with lots of funds marked NL, or no-load. Then after obtaining the toll-free telephone numbers of the various companies from 1-800-555-1212, call to find out about their services, making a point of getting the following information:

Ask about switching privileges offered by the fund manager. Toll-free telephone calls, instant switching without the need for paperwork, fees, minimums, and so forth.

Ask for a prospectus on each fund in the family that potentially interests you. You should also request the "Statement of Additional Information" for each. The discount brokers will usually send you just three prospectuses, but you can request others directly from the funds. These will show you the stated purpose of the fund (high-potential/high-risk, for example) and give you a record of its past performance.

Make sure that the selection of funds in the family is right for you. If you are in a high income bracket you will want a family with a good selection of tax-exempt funds—long-term, money market, and state-tax-exempt bonds for your state. If you are using the switching technique for your IRA, you will want a wide selection of interest-generating funds such as long- and short-term bond funds, Ginnie Mae funds and money market funds, since tax protection on interest income is one of the greatest benefits of your IRA.

Check the services offered by the management company. Most offer check writing privileges on non-IRA accounts and permit you to select the option of having dividends automatically reinvested. Some also offer monthly payroll deduction through your bank account.

Some discount brokers also offer instant telephone trades for mutual funds, and Charles Schwab & Co., for example, handles more than 100 no-load funds. Fees for switching are comparable to commissions on stock transactions—for example, it would cost you $20, or 2%, to acquire $1000 in shares of a mutual fund handled by Schwab and another $20 to swap those shares for $1000 in another fund. The advantage of opening your account with a discount broker is that you can move among fund families—from a Fidelity fund to a Dreyfus one, for example.

Now that you have an account for switching, how do you decide when and where to switch? The fact is that no one is a soothsayer who can always be in the right place at the right time, not even investment professionals. But in the investment markets there are ways to improve your odds just like there are at cards. You may not be 100% accurate about when to sell General Motors and buy into the smokestack stocks, but at least you can boost your odds by getting out of the stock market when it's dropping, and getting into gold when its price is rising.

Let's look at some specific market conditions: In late July of 1982 interest rates were falling sharply. As returns dropped, several timing newsletters suggested investors begin moving money out of money market funds and into Blue Chip stocks, based more on the increasing unattractiveness of money market interest rates than any promise of a hot stock market in the near future. If you had moved some of your investment money into the stock market before August 1982, you would have caught the stock market's meteoric upturn. The Dow Jones industrial average moved from under 800 to more than 1000 by year-end 1982. Fortunes were made by some of the professionals, but most individuals left their money in the familiar money market funds or even savings accounts until 1983 or even 1984, when the Dow Jones average flattened and fell back. Even if you missed the precise moment of the August 1982 market turn, you might have moved into the rising market the following month—if you had been watching closely or if you had subscribed to a timing newsletter—and you would still have benefitted by getting into the market in September or October.

The point is that you need some idea of market cycles. You don't need to anticipate turns in markets to make substantial profits. You only need to know that a turn in a cycle has occurred. Some investors use the rule of thumb that a market has "turned" if the price or rate has moved up at least 10% from a "bottom"—a rise to 7.7% from 7.0% for 90-day Treasury Bill rates, for example. By charting market cycles on your own, you can at least avoid big, long-lasting mistakes. If you want professional help in determining the cycles and moment to switch, there are dozens of market timing services and newsletters that give you model portfolios broken down into various types of funds and tell you when to switch from one type of fund to another. Some of these services will do the switching for you for a fee.

"The Switch Fund Advisory," a weekly and monthly newsletter service from Schabacker Investment Management (301-840-0301) in Gaithersburg, Md., uses twenty-six technical variables to come up with its model portfolio each week. Major changes in the portfolio come every few months.

Dick Fabian's "Telephone Switch Newsletter" (800-772-7272) in Huntington Beach, Calif., on the other hand, does not specify which portion of the investment should be in cash or money market funds but concentrates on the breakdown of holdings among bonds, stocks, stock sectors such as international funds, and gold.

Another is "Systems and Forecasts," a weekly newsletter and twice-a-week telephone hotline service from Signalert Corp. (516-829-6444) Great Neck, New York.

None of these newsletters are cheap. Most cost between $100 and $200 a year. But the three named here aim for—and generally have achieved over the past few years—annual returns of 20% or more on your investment. And that's definitely better than you would have done if you had simply parked all your money in a money market fund or Certificate of Deposit. You can reduce the cost of such a service by sharing a newsletter subscription with several friends or even setting up a little investment club to share the cost.

Whether you chart your own market cycles using the 10% turn rule-of-thumb, the interest rate thermometer described in Chapter 6, a market timing service, or all three, it makes sense to keep your eye on the market cycles and move your money around. But whatever you do, remember to select your mutual funds because you expect them to perform well in the near future, not because they were top performers in the past. Market conditions change. If you had checked newspaper and magazine rankings of performance for mutual funds each quarter or year and moved all your money into the top-ranked fund for the next quarter, your performance would have been dismal. You would be getting into exactly what you should be getting out of.

After you select your mutual fund family, you should carefully study prospectuses for each of the available funds. But when you are at the selection stage the names and types of funds can get confusing. Here are some rough guidelines to help you identify the type of a mutual fund if all you know about it is the name as it appears in the listing of your daily newspaper or in magazine articles where the funds are ranked.

Stock funds. The following types usually invest in the stock market: emerging growth and growth funds (stocks of small and emerging companies—high potential risk, high potential reward); equity income and income funds (stocks that pay large dividends and are less likely to show large capital gains than the average stock); average performance funds and balanced funds (stocks picked because they are representative of a cross section of the stock market or because the high-risk ones are offset by more stable issues.)

Stock market segments. Energy funds, natural resources, gold, international and foreign stocks, etc.

Money market funds. Funds are available that invest primarily in government securities, institutional securities or even just Treasury Bills. In addition, many fund families have tax-exempt money market funds.

Bond funds. Mutual funds are available that invest in corporate bonds and in government bonds of various maturities; the high-yield funds generally invest in such things as junk bonds or state-insured Certificates of Deposit, giving them a higher yield than other bond funds but increasing the risk.

12

Selecting Brokers, Bankers and Agents

When you choose an investment advisor, you are really making two choices; you are selecting the institution with which you will be doing business as well as the specific individual at that firm with whom you will generally deal.

Of course, with some types of institutions, such as the mutual fund families mentioned in the last chapter or big discount brokers, you do not deal with specific individuals. You opt for the lower trading fees and electronic services over the benefits of doing business with a live human being. Some investors find this way of doing business without someone to offer advice and talk over ideas to be discomforting. Such investors should shun electronic trading, discount brokers, and mutual fund switching families. But make no mistake, you pay for advice and chitchat in the investment world today whether or not you see the full cost on your monthly statement. Thus, if you value human contact or feel research and investment advice are essential to you, it makes sense to shop long and hard for these costly services.

Most stockbrokers, insurance agents, financial planners, and commodities representatives are really salesmen, who are paid a commission on your business. Their firms are also involved in selling products and services to you, and the big spender is likely to get more attention than the little IRA investor with $500.

It's getting a little tricky these days, telling an insurance company from a bank or a brokerage service. Time was when a securities brokerage firm was a securities broker, period. No longer. Over the past decade brokerage firms have acquired everything from insurance companies to mutual fund distributors. At the same time, the brokerage firms are themselves being gobbled up by banks and big corporations like American Express or Sears Roebuck, both owning an assortment of brokers and other financial subsidiaries.

The result is a bunch of financial cafeterias. The stockbroker from Shearson Lehman (an American Express subsidiary) who puts you into the stock market can also offer insurance from Fireman's Fund (another American Express unit) or mutual funds from the company's IDS Services unit. In fact, most big financial firms—whether they were originally insurance companies, securities brokers or banks—now offer a wide range of financial products through a sales force that you may think of as stockbrokers, financial planners, or insurance agents. In reality, however, these salesmen are becoming interchangeable, and all are just about equally ready to sell you the same types of financial products.

SECURITIES BOUTIQUES

Does that mean the old-fashioned stockbroker has disappeared? No, you can still find one-product brokers in many regional brokerage firms. And some big brokers who mass-market over-the-counter stocks and new issues have entire boiler rooms of brokers on the phone selling just these products.

To locate a regional broker it is useful to consult Standard & Poor's *Security Dealers of North America*, an annual dictionary of all of the nation's brokerage firms broken down by region. Most public libraries have it.

Regional brokers tend to be weak on research in the big exchange-listed stocks, but they often have useful research on local companies, particularly small ones that trade over-the-counter. And if you decide to make a big investment in tax-exempt municipal bonds, regional brokers are often the best source.

DEALING WITH A SALESMAN

Unless you decide to do business with a regional broker or securities boutique, chances are you'll be dealing with an all-purpose financial product salesman, regardless of what hat he happens to be wearing. How do you go about shopping for such a person? For one thing, you should not open an account with a brokerage house just because a broker happens to call you on the phone with a hot salespitch for several stocks he's pushing. That's how most brokerage accounts are opened. It's called "prospecting" in the business. The practice produces "leads" for securities brokers—just like inexpensive computerized financial plans do.

There's nothing wrong with "prospecting," or opening a brokerage account with the "financial planner" who calls as a follow-up to your "financial plan." It's just that a savvy investor—if he actually intends to invest in securities—should shop around a bit before opening an account. Compare rates and services, for example.

SHOPPING FOR A BROKER OR PLANNER

The first thing to do is contact a number of big financial institutions to find out what products and services are available. Whether you reach them through their advertising, direct mail solicitations, or by looking up the main office in your telephone book, you can be certain a salesman will promptly be assigned to follow up. What's more, most big brokerage firms and fund families have 800-numbers that you can quickly obtain from 800-555-1212.

At first you should pay more attention to the company and its products than the individual who has contacted you. If research is what interests you, find out what sort of research the firm makes available to interested individuals. Does the firm have research analysts in the areas that interest you—be they energy stocks, over-the-counter stocks, or municipal bonds? Can you, as a small investor, get quick access to the research analysts' reports and buy-and-sell recommendations? If the analyst recommends selling a security in your portfolio, are you assured that the information will reach you quickly, if not immediately.

You will also want to assess its other services. Is the institution equipped to move you from one investment to another with a telephone call? Does it offer a broad range of investment products that are of interest to you, including, say, financial planning, tax advice or free checking against your non-IRA investment accounts?

Assuming you find an institution that seems to offer what you want, you are ready to select your individual contact at that institution. Your first goal is to find someone who truly understands and follows investment areas that interest you. While all of the salesmen at the brokerage may be Registered Representatives, which means they have passed a fairly rigid examination on the workings of the securities markets and registered with the National Association of Securities Dealers, not everyone is a specialist in hot little OTC stocks, government agency bond funds, or index options. Match the broker you select with your special interests.

The personality of your broker is another important consideration—if the two of you get along well, you'll probably get better service and more information—but remember, his expertise is more important. It doesn't matter what a company offers if your salesman doesn't understand the products that are most suitable for you.

If you end up with someone wearing the hat of a financial planner, he may or may not be a Registered Representative. The problem with the current financial planner boom is that "financial planner" is a generic term like florist or student. And while colleges of financial planning are turning out graduates who are specialists, not all are members of the International Association for Financial Planning (IAFP), which has a qualifying exam. The IAFP is attempting, without much success, to push through a national accrediting procedure to assure that anyone using the financial planner title would be compelled to qualify for and join a professional organization.

The SEC has warned that all who call themselves financial planners and give investment advice must register as investment advisers. However, all that is required of them by the SEC at this time is that they fill out a basic form and pay a fee. Many states also register planners who give investment advice.

Meanwhile, insurance companies, banks and other institutions are setting up financial planning departments and courses for their agents and officers at a rapid clip. Since there are no educational requirements nor tests to give some assurance of the expertise of these salesman, your best guide is your own judgment of how knowledgeable or comfortable the "planner" seems to be with various types of investments and with you. If you get even the slightest feeling you're being hustled, back off.

It is possible to get investment advice and financial planning from professionals who aren't salesmen, but good financial advice is very expensive—and poor financial advice is also expensive. Often the two are hard to tell apart. A number of IAFP members are fee-only financial planners or planners who won't sell you directly any securities, tax shelters or other investments. Some work for financial planning services which are directed to the needs of wealthy individuals and often provided by corporations as a benefit to their top managers. A clue to the real cost of financial advice, such services generally cost at least $5000 a year and can cost more than $15,000.

Besides the independent consultants, financial institutions frequently offer such services; bank trust departments, most brokerage houses, and commodities brokers offer managed accounts, and even some of the publishers of investment newsletters will take over management of your funds for a fee. Few such services are available, however, for accounts smaller than $100,000.

SHOPPING FOR A COMMODITIES BROKER

No area is trickier for investors than commodities. And while there are a number of commodities houses that specialize in the futures market, you are probably better off sticking with the commodities departments of brokerage houses, where representatives must be registered with the SEC.

Boiler rooms for commodity schemes directed at little investors flourished in the late 1970's. The most fraudulent were ultimately cleaned up by the Commodities Futures Trading Commission—the government agency that is to commodities markets what the SEC is to securities—but most commodities salesmen operating outside the brokerage houses still have not been screened for education or expertise. Until 1984 a person could sell commodities as an "Associated Person" (AP) merely by filing his name with the CFTC, paying a $15 fee, and avowing he had never committed a felony. Now AP candidates must pass the National Futures Assocation test, which is a version of an exam given to members of the Chicago Board of Trade, a big commodities exchange. But AP's that began selling commodities before the spring of 1984 need not take the exam to remain registered. And many of the old boiler room telephone pitches are still being peddled by the APs, although most today are at least on the right side of the law.

An alternative way to buy commodities is through commodities discount brokers who advertise their services daily on the commodities pages of the *Wall Street Journal*. For the most part these discount brokers—like their counterparts in the securities industry—offer little research or guidance to the commodities investor.

ACCOUNTANTS AND LAWYERS

Most reasonably wealthy investors have their own accountant and their own lawyer. For the little investor the use of these professionals makes sense under certain circumstances. Lawyers are needed for setting up Keogh plans, Clifford trusts, and other complex investment structures. Tax lawyers are particularly helpful in helping you find ways to shelter income, although the little investor will find nearly comparable advice in most of the inexpensive computerized financial plans.

It is also useful to have a lawyer look at the prospectus for any tax shelter or investment scheme you might have in mind. The purpose of this professional scrutiny is to judge the legality of such a scheme rather than its potential profitability. There is, however, no better way to spot a scam that could cost you money than to tell the promoter you can't sign or buy until after your lawyer scans the offering material. If the promoter responds to such a statement with an almost hysterical effort to get you to sign immediately, back off. As for professional advice on the potential profitability of a tax shelter or investment scheme, you might do better to consult a Certified Public Accountant (CPA). But watch out. On products like limited partnership tax shelters it's not uncommon for an intermediary such as an accountant to get a fee in excess of 20% of the initial cash investment. In fact, accountants were the original financial planners for the rich.

13

Opening Margin Accounts

Securities. You can't buy stocks or bonds on margin for your Individual Retirement Account, but there is no such restriction on borrowing to buy securities outside your IRA. You can borrow money to buy stocks or bonds in much the same way you take an automobile loan from a car dealer—you make a down payment and borrow the rest from your broker. What's more, some discount brokers will lend at rates lower than a bank would charge you for an auto or personal loan.

Little investors are usually cautioned about the risks in margin buying, although the process is widely used by sophisticated investors and professionals. Without question the risks are greater than for straight purchases of stock. When you buy on margin you can lose more than you put up. If, for example, you put up $2000 to buy $4000 of stock, borrowing the additional $2000 from your broker, you could be out more than your $2000 if the stock price plummeted low enough, since you would also have to repay the loan. Along the way you could get some "margin calls" from your broker if the price of your stock dropped below 25% of its initial price. At that point you must put more money or security in your margin account or sell some of the shares to raise money so that your cash investment meets margin requirements.

What are margin requirements? The Federal Reserve Board—the government agency that runs the nation's banks—sets the maximum you may borrow, which cur-

SETTING UP YOUR INVESTMENT ACCOUNTS

rently is 50% of the purchase price of your securities. There have been times in the last few decades that the FED set the margin requirement, as it is called, at 100%, in effect prohibiting borrowing for purchase of securities when it felt a risky situation could be developing. Margin has been at 50% for stocks and convertible securities since 1974, but you can borrow as much as two-thirds of the money to buy regular bonds on margin.

It pays to shop around for the best interest rate on loans from your broker. Securities brokers charge their customers rates pegged to the going rate for call money, which is quoted daily in the money rates table of the *Wall Street Journal*. Call money quotes are the rates banks charge on loans to brokers against stock exchange collateral—in this case your stocks. Since they are collateralized, such broker loans generally carry rates several points beneath the Prime Rate which banks charge for unsecured loans to their most credit-worthy customers. Most brokers charge their margin customers from one percentage point to three percentage points over the rate for call money. It does you little good to negotiate with your broker for a better rate, but rates do vary substantially from brokerage house to brokerage house, with some securities houses charging lower rates for large transactions. What's more, some discount brokers like Rose & Co.—the unit of the Chase Manhattan Bank—charge just 0.5% over the brokers' call money rate.

Opening a margin account is relatively easy, whether you use a full-service broker or a discount broker. Most require you to fill out an application and sign an agreement. The application is less complicated than forms for many credit cards. The agreement specifies that the broker can keep your shares in a "street name" and sell them, if you miss margin calls, to pay back the money you were lent for the initial purchase. The New York Stock Exchange requires you to put up a minimum of $2000 to open a margin account. Once the account is open, however, you can order on credit with a telephone call.

Should you have a margin account? Probably not if you are a small investor, and particularly not if you have any bent toward gambling. If your primary investments are in Individual Retirement Accounts your trustee won't let you trade through a margin account. It is against the law to borrow against securities in an IRA. But if stock-market investing outside your IRA is a big part of your investment plan, you should consider this alternative.

Commodities. Margin accounts for trading commodities futures are quite different than those for securities. Your commodities broker does not lend you any money, which is why it is technically legal to hold commodities futures in a margin account for your IRA. As a practical matter, however, it's hard to imagine a good reason for doing so. Because of margin calls and the possible need to put up more money, you could run afoul of the $2000 maximum IRA annual limit if your contracts weren't properly hedged.

Your margin deposit—which is usually between 4% and 20% of the value of a commodities contract—is basically a security deposit. Neither you nor your commodities broker must put up any more money until the contract is settled, or your apparent losses would appear to exceed the deposit. If so, you get a margin call to put up additional funds. The amount of security deposit you must put up at any given time is set by the exchange on which the commodity trades. It is a flat dollar amount, for example, the New York Commodity Exchange (CMX) requires a $1400 deposit for a standard gold contract of 100 troy ounces regardless of the point price of gold.

14

Comparing Rates and Services

How much do you save by doing business with a discount broker? Various amounts, depending on what kind of discount broker you select and what you are willing to give up in exchange for lower fees.

In these days of financial cafeterias, some of the large discount brokers, like Fidelity Investments of Boston or Charles Schwab & Co., offer not only a full line of securities—stocks, options, foreign securities, bonds including zero-coupon bonds, mutual funds, and so forth—but they also supply their customers with stock quotes over 800-numbers and supply computer research services. Such brokers are generally equipped to open an Individual Retirement Account for you just like the full-service brokers. About the only difference between the big discount firms and the full-service brokers, like Merrill Lynch or E. F. Hutton, is that the discounters don't give you their own advice and guidance; they sell you access to research through your computer, to advice from others (see Part VII). And, of course, their fees and commissions are lower.

These big, multiple-line discount brokers will generally fill a small order—say $300 shares at $30 a share—for about half what the full-service brokers would charge. Schwab would charge $89 compared to $180 at Hutton. The difference between the two types on bigger orders like 1000 shares for a total of $30,000 is even more striking. Hutton would charge $490 and Schwab, less than a third of that—$144.

But these discounters tag on minimum fees per trade of $30–$35, which the full-service firms don't charge. So on a tiny order like 100 shares of a $5 stock, the big discounters might charge more.

Nor are the big full-product discounters the only price cutters on the block. If it is rates you want, check with brokers who charge you by the share—like Whitehall Securities in New York or Pacific Brokerage Services in Los Angeles. Such companies don't offer much besides stocks and bonds and they don't have fancy computer services, but they're cheap. They don't have minimums for little trades, and Pacific Brokerage will trade three hundred $30 shares for just $25—less than a third of Schwab's rate and miniscule when compared with $193 charges by Merrill Lynch for the same trade. On orders of high-price stocks the rate cutters are even more enticing. Pacific will do 400 shares at $90 for a fee of $35. That compares with $388 for Merrill Lynch and $156 for Schwab.

Moreover, many of these super rate-cutters are equipped to act as custodian for IRAs. The point is that brokers are getting very competitive, and that's good for you. By shopping around you can get exactly what you want to pay for. If it's expert advice, you pay for advice; if it's convenience and being able to switch with a phone call from one investment to another—as you can do at Fidelity and Schwab—you pay for that.

Spear Securities, the firm that's doing 24-hour trading by making markets in certain stocks, has rates in the same range as Schwab and Fidelity (see Chapter 37).

15
Restitution: Getting Your Money Back

Despite your care in selecting a securities broker or dealer or commodities account manager, sometimes things go wrong. Perhaps you suspect that your stock broker has enriched himself at your expense. Or you bought into a mutual fund hawking 17% returns and you got only 2%.

If you get mad at your broker, you're not alone. Consumer complaints to the Securities & Exchange Commission hit a record 15,000 in 1984. Complaints going to arbitration in the same year were up more than 40% from the prior year. And an increasing number of angry investors are taking their brokers to court. The most common complaints: churning (excessive buying and selling to generate maximum commissions); putting unsophisticated clients into investments that were too risky or completely unsuitable for their needs; and gross exaggeration of the potential for gain along with deliberate underemphasis of the potential risk in an investment.

WHERE TO COMPLAIN

Here's how to complain and get results: Start with the commodities salesman or Registered Representative who was your broker, and if that doesn't help, move on and complain to the branch manager of your brokerage firm. If the matter isn't handled to your satisfaction, you should make clear to the branch manager—in writing—the exact nature of your complaint and what you intend to do next.

In any matter involving securities—whether stocks, stock options or bonds—the Securities & Exchange Commission, an agency of the Federal government, is the authority. Send your letter of complaint, along with copies of letters you have addressed to the branch manager, to:

> Enforcement Division
> Securities & Exchange Commission
> 450 Fifth St., N.W.
> Washington, D.C. 20549

As a practical matter the SEC regulates the brokers and dealers and has power to investigate them, but you may fare better as an individual complainant if you contact someone who is equipped to handle problems on a case-by-case basis. If your complaint involves a brokerage firm that is a member of the New York Stock Exchange, you can complain directly to the Exchange. As with a complaint to the SEC send copies of the letters you wrote to the firm's branch manager along with your letter of complaint to:

> The New York Stock Exchange
> Investor-Broker Liaison
> 55 Water Street
> New York, N.Y. 10041

The Exchange can put your complaint into arbitration, which is cheaper and faster than filing suit against your broker. Before you consent to arbitration, however, seek legal counsel, since consenting to arbitration can affect your right to sue. (From the time you first open an account with your broker, you should anticipate such a situation arising and protect your right to go to court by resisting any attempt by your broker to get you to sign an agreement that restricts you to settling complaints against the firm by arbitration. You can always opt for arbitration when a dispute arises, but you're also free to take the matter to court.)

If your brokerage house is not a member of the NYSE, you should file your complaint and seek arbitration through the National Association of Securities Dealers at the following address:

> Surveillance Department
> National Association of Securities Dealers
> 1735 K Street, N.W.
> Washington, D.C. 20006

It is a good idea to send a copy of any complaint you have to the NASD regardless of how—and through what agency—you attempt to proceed. The NASD, a private organization funded by the securities dealers, exists as a result of Federal legislation and is overseen by the SEC. Its powers include the authority to help you resolve your differences with your broker and to discipline securities firms and individuals. Beyond that, the NASD also has arbitration panels similar to the NYSE panels that can force the firms to return money to you. If your case involves less than $5000, it is usually arbitrated by a single arbitrator—a lawyer or law professor assigned to your case by the NASD or NYSE. Where more money is involved, a three-member panel of arbitrators is appointed, with at least two coming from outside the securities industry. The NASD can get involved regardless of whether your problem involves stocks, government or commercial bonds, or other securities. And about 51% of the cases that go to NASD arbitration result in some restitution for the customer.

You can also complain to the NASD if mutual funds and mutual fund management companies are the source of your problem. That's because the mutual fund's distributor—whether a mutual fund management company distributes its own funds or farms out the task to other distributors—must be a member of the NASD. In these cases be sure to include in your complaint the identity of the person and firm who actually sold you the mutual fund shares as well as the name of the fund and mutual fund management company.

For complaints pertaining to mutual funds you can also contact the securities department of the attorney general's office for the state in which the fund is licensed. These offices are usually based in the state capitol.

If municipal bonds are the subject of your complaint you should contact:

> The Municipal Securities Rule-Making Board
> Suite 800
> 1818 N Street, N.W.
> Washington, D.C. 20036

If the investment product causing the problem was sold to you by an insurance company, write to the insurance department in your state capitol, since insurance companies are primarily state regulated.

Commodities futures and options are regulated by the Commodities Futures Trading Commission, a government agency which regulates commodities firms, salesmen, and markets, much like the SEC oversees securities. Complaints filed with the CFTC may be handled out of one of their regional offices, but the best place to write is CFTC headquarters at the following address:

> Commodities Futures Trading Commission
> 2033 K Street, N.W.
> Washington, D.C. 20581

The commodities industry's self-policing arm is the National Futures Association, based in New York City. Send copies of your complaint to the NFA as well as to any commodities exchanges on which your futures contracts were supposedly traded.

SETTING UP YOUR INVESTMENT ACCOUNTS

If your complaint is with a savings and loan, write to:

> Office of Community Investments
> Federal Home Loan Bank Board
> 1700 G St., N.W.
> Washington, D.C. 20552

And if your problem is with a Federally chartered commercial bank you should write to the closest office of the Controller of the Currency. The offices are located in Atlanta, Chicago, Dallas, Kansas City, New York City, and San Francisco. If the bank is state chartered, you should contact the following agencies:

> Office of Community Investments
> Federal Home Loan Bank Board
> 1700 G St., N.W.
> Washington, D.C. 20552
>
> Division of Consumer and Community Affairs
> Federal Reserve Board
> Washington, D.C. 20551

When you decide to file a formal complaint relating to any type of investment, don't write to just one of the suggested organizations and agencies; write to any that you feel might have any interest in your case and send the letters all at once. If weeks pass and you get no response, send a followup letter or make a phone call. In instances where fraud is suspected—whether in mutual funds, stocks, or bonds—the attorney general's office in any state involved should be sent copies of your letters of complaint.

GOING TO COURT

In certain instances the courts are the right place to take your complaint. In 1985 the Supreme Court affirmed your right to sue your broker if he gave you a hot tip—or theoretical inside information—that proved to be false, causing you to lose money. The Court ruled that if the information was false, then it wasn't true "inside information" under the law; thus you, the customer, hadn't violated the law. "Inside information" is potential news about a public company that one receives before it is available to the general public. If the news is considered "material," it is illegal for an "insider" to buy or sell the shares involved before the information is publicly available. Trading on such inside information, if it is valid, is punishable by treble damages (you must pay to the court three times your profits), and by an enjoinment that could subject you to a jail sentence if you violate insider trading laws again.

But fake hot tips aren't the only complaint you can take to the courts. Some lawyers now are specializing in investor lawsuits as evidenced by an advertisement placed in the *Wall Street Journal* last year by one law firm: "Have you lost money because you were misled? If you have been deceived in the purchase of a publicly traded stock, a private placement, a tax shelter, or have been treated unfairly by a company you have invested in, you may be able to take legal action to recover your losses," was the message of the ad.

Most cases involving account churning and unsuitable investments are settled out of court—probably resulting in larger damage settlements than those handled through arbitration. On the other hand, it is substantially more expensive to sue than to arbitrate.

PART III

Ways to Earn Interest

From a practical standpoint—as explained in Part I—it makes sense to invest your IRA money heavily, if not totally, in securities that pay interest.

The basic forms of interest-rate-paying investments are short-term money-market vehicles like money market accounts, Certificates of Deposit, and Treasury Bills as well as long-term bonds.

For years investors viewed bonds as a highly conservative investment, a place where you parked your money and raked in a nice—far from greedy—return over the years. But during the past ten years interest rates have been so volatile and bond prices have whipsawed so sharply that cautious investors became distressed, particularly when they saw the market value of their safe-and-sure bonds—in periods of rising interest rates—plummet to a fraction of their face value.

From the standpoint of your IRA, such gyrations in resale prices don't really matter unless you sell the bonds before they mature. Even for your IRA, however, it makes sense to park in the short-term money market when rates are low and then invest long-term when rates are high. The best time to enter the long-term bond market is when rates are high or just beginning to fall from a high point. That's when you can lock in for a long time at a high rate, assuring decades of returns of 16% or more on your money. Beyond that, if rates outside your bond then begin to fall, the value or price at which you can sell your bond, rises proportionally.

It's often tempting, however, to buy long-term bonds when rates are generally low, since the rates they offer are at least higher than those in your money market account or that you can get for a six-month or year-long Certificate of Deposit. And, indeed, when your money market account is returning 7%, it hardly seems the way to accumulate the money you will need for retirement in your IRA. So if rates are low but you still are determined to buy long-term bonds, it clearly makes sense to shop around for the best rate. Study carefully the various types of bonds and how return varies with different maturities and degrees of risk. (See Chapter 16 for a discussion on this subject.)

One problem with buying a long-term bond for your IRA when rates are low is that when interest rates go back up—and long-term securities historically top 13% every three or four years—you'll be locked in at 10% or 11%. Another problem is that should you have to sell the bond before it matures and at a time when interest rates are on the high side, you will have to sell at a price lower than you paid for the bond. That's what's tricky about bonds. As interest rates in general rise the value, or selling price, of a bond falls. As a result, basic bond investment strategy is to buy long-term bonds when rates are very high and sell them when rates are at their bottom, which is when you can get prices much higher than you paid.

The usual strategy of professionals is to invest at low rates in short-term securities (similar to your money market account) until rates begin hit high levels and then buy more long-term bonds. This strategy has rarely if ever been suggested for individuals with IRAs on the grounds that they could end up with a lower total return. But odds are that if you repeat this strategy each time long-term rates rise or fall, you will substantially increase your average return and, hence, the amount of money available to you for retirement.

16

Risk Versus Reward

There are a number of ways to get returns that are higher than those paid by Certificates of Deposit. In the "Pick-a-rate" IRA strategy outlined in Chapter 5, what you vary—from market to market—is "risk" to get the rate you need. Here is a look at other ways of increasing your current return either by investing longer or by switching to a less secure type of investment.

Changing the time. In most markets you can get a better return on three- to five-year Certificates of Deposit from your bank, or a Treasury Note or Bond with a maturity of three years or more, than you can in your money market fund or with ninety-day Treasury Bills. The disadvantage is that you may be locked into your investment when interest rates again hit high levels. You can always sell your Treasury securities, but if rates rise, the market value will fall sharply.

Conversely, when interest rates are very high, short-term rates often rise to levels higher than those for long-term securities. The reason for this is that at high-rate times everyone wants to lock in for as long as possible, and investors must be offered an incentive to invest in short-term securities. When that happens, the danger is that you will get locked out just when long-term rates are the highest because you are coasting along in a three-year Certificate of Deposit or Treasury Note. You won't have that problem if you stick to a money market fund where you are permitted to withdraw your money without penalty.

Increasing the risk. Yield is always related to risk; the greater the risk, the greater the return. Long-term Treasury Bonds returning, say, 10% are totally safe, since they are backed by the U.S. Government. Certificates of Deposit at banks insured by the Federal Deposit Insurance Corp. (FDIC) are also secure. As a result these securities pay the lowest long-term returns around. But venture out into a state-insured Certificate of Deposit from an out-of-state bank that's not Federally insured, and you can get rates that are 2 or 3 percentage points higher. At a risk of course—there have been runs on some out-of-state banks that did not have Federal insurance. Investors may eventually get their money back, but not without a nasty scare.

Here's a ballpark look at how rates generally shape up relative to each other. For purposes of this example, assume Treasury Bill rates—the safest, shortest-term, and lowest-paying security—are around 7% putting the base rate at a low level. When rates generally rise, all will rise proportionately, based on relative risk. Long-term rates aren't as volatile as short-term ones, however, and when overall rates are peaking at a very high level, sometimes— for a brief period—short rates are higher than long ones.

The bonds mentioned in the rates comparison presented below can all be purchased through securities brokers, and many can be acquired through your bank.

Government National Mortgage Association Securities (Ginnie Maes). Due in one-year—1 percentage point higher than the Treasury Bill base rate; due in two-and-a-half years—2 points higher; due in six years or more— 3 or more points higher. These government agency securities pay slightly higher interest than Treasury Bonds and are backed by the U.S. Government.

Corporate and Utility Bonds. Top-rated utility bonds at present return around 4 to 5 percentage points more than Treasury Bills. Top-rated corporate bonds yield some 4 percentage points over the Treasury Bill base rate.

Baa-rated bonds (the lowest investment-quality grade) yield around 5 percentage points more than Treasury Bills. There are also high-risk, so-called junk bonds, which might yield as much as 7 percentage points above the base.

In general, individuals should not venture into bonds with anything but A's in the rating. You may not wipe out with a Baa-rated bond, but it's advisable to leave this risk to the professionals, or to buy them only as part of a diversified bond fund. (See ratings at the end of this chapter.)

With long-term bonds you not only have to worry about the underlying security, if it's not Federally guaranteed, but you must worry about the basic value. When interest rates rise, the price at which you can resell your bond will fall. If your bond is a zero-coupon, which means it doesn't make interest payments along the way, its price decline will be even steeper than an ordinary coupon-paying bond. In short, don't buy long-term bonds for your IRA when rates are low unless you intend to hold onto them until maturity.

For a short-term strategy when rates are low and holding, you might consider the following, but only if you can stand some risk and are willing to keep a day-to-day watch on mutual fund quotations in your daily newspaper.

Playing the funds. Long-term bond mutual funds that you can switch into and out of with a telephone call are relatively new. Today the yields are about the same as yields for long-term bonds. So why not use them like money market accounts when overall rates are low. You could lock in the higher yield until rates in short-term money market funds climb higher than the yield you locked in. If, for example, you lock in a yield of 10.5%, no matter what happens to rates the yield of your mutual fund shares will remain around 10.5%. Say rates for long-term bonds of comparable quality rise to 12%. The current yield of your bond mutual fund would also rise—but only for new investors.

The trick, of course, is that shares of such funds behave a little bit like bonds. When interest rates begin to rise, the price of the bond shares—or asset value—starts to fall just like bond prices do. Let's say that on June 7, 1985, you had bought $5000 of shares in Fidelity's Thrift Trust, its fund of high-quality long-term corporate bonds yielding around 11%. At that day's asset price of $10.49 you would have purchased about 477 shares. In the following month, long-term interest rates generally rose slightly. By early July you would have collected a month's worth of interest—slightly less than $50. But the asset value of your shares, since outside rates rose a tiny bit, had fallen to $10.34, reducing the value of your 477 shares to $4928. Thus, you would actually have lost money during the month, which can't happen to you in an insured money market account. Of course, exactly the opposite would have occurred had rates edged off a bit and asset-value-per-share increased. You not only would have collected the yield but also would have had a capital gain on the value of your shares.

As long as interest rates stay at low levels or drop further, a short-term investment in long-term bond fund shares might make sense. One strategy might be to set a floor on asset-value-per-share. Determine in advance that if your shares drop a given percentage below your purchase price you will immediately sell, taking a small loss and moving your money back into your money market account. Since many of these long-term funds are no-load—meaning you pay no up-front fee to get in—and because many management companies charge no fee for switching, your risk is at least limited to any decline in asset value.

Your stockbroker can usually only sell you shares of his own firm's long-term bond fund and these frequently carry a "load." To buy shares directly from a fund management company, find the manager's name in the daily mutual fund quotation listings in your newspaper and locate the company by calling 800-555-1212. Most mutual fund families have a number of different types of long-term bond funds. While individual Baa bonds may be too risky for small investors, it can make sense over the short term to invest in middle-rated corporate bond funds if you decide to play the bond-fund-switching game. Not only do such bond funds pay much higher returns but buying these riskier securities in a fund spreads out your exposure and reduces the risk that a single security will wipe you out if it goes bad. Beyond that, any risk in bond grade is overshadowed by the real risk that asset value of your shares will fall.

To determine the quality of bonds offered to you—whether they are commercial bonds or even municipals—check standard bond agency ratings. For purposes of comparison, Federal government-backed bonds would be AAA+ if they were rated—which they aren't since they are guaranteed by the U.S. government. Little investors are always advised to stick to bonds with only As in the ratings. While that makes sense in terms of individual bond issues, there is less risk if you buy shares of a mutual fund made up of bond issues of Baa and lower.

Bond Ratings:

Standard & Poor's	Moody's	Yield differences	Quality
AAA	Aaa	lowest yield	Extremely strong

WAYS TO EARN INTEREST

AA	AA	¼% better than AAA	Very strong
A	A	½% better than AA	Strong
BBB	Baa	⅞% better than A	Adequate
BB	BA	2% better and more as quality drops	Increasingly speculative; C and D rated may not pay dividends
B	BA		
CCC	Caa		
CC	CC		
C	C		
D	D		

17

Money Market Accounts

By now, everyone knows about money market accounts. Whether you open a money market deposit account at a bank or savings and loan, or put your money into a money market fund run by a mutual fund management company, the benefits outpace the old savings account by a wide margin.

Before the early 1970s when money market accounts emerged, the money markets were pretty much the unchallenged province of big institutional investors. The Treasury Bills, commercial paper and bankers' acceptances, which the large financial institutions like banks and insurance companies employ to lend and borrow money among themselves and back and forth to the Federal government, come only in $10,000 chunks or bigger. However, by using the mutual fund idea—pooling lots of money market securities and selling the shares to little investors in little pieces—this highly sophisticated institutional market suddenly came into the range of everyone. The banks and brokerage houses keep buying new money market investments as the old ones mature—thus the little investor can deposit money in such a fund, which ends up working much like a high-interest savings account.

Whether you open your account with a bank or have your fund as part of a mutual fund family, the benefits are roughly the same—checking privileges for non-IRA accounts (although there can be restrictions on the number of checks you can write each month at banks or on the size of your checks in mutual funds) and yield that's higher than you could get in an ordinary savings account. If you open your account at a Federally insured bank or savings and loan, your money is insured up to the Federal limit, currently $100,000. But most mutual fund companies buy private insurance, so these funds are usually insured as well. Often mutual funds will have minimum limits on the size of your initial deposit—it can't be less than $1000. Savings and loans by law once required even larger minimum deposits, but that changed at the end of 1985.

In comparing rates offered by money market accounts you will sometimes see a published figure that is identified in the footnotes as current annual yield. Advertisers have at times incorrectly identified this type of rate as annual interest paid by a fund. But there is a significant difference between interest and yield, and the two should not be confused. The interest rate is the total amount of interest the fund is able to pay its shareholders, based on the cumulative interest paid by the securities in the fund minus any management fees and expenses. Yield, on the other hand, reflects the pace at which the interest is compounded—daily, weekly, monthly, or even semiannually. Each time the interest is compounded, you get a bit better return because you are collecting interest on the previously compounded interest. As a result a fund paying interest at an annual rate of 10% might have a current annual yield of, say, 10.5%. It is usually best to compare yield to yield, since that is what you actually collect. Rates and yields on long-term bonds, by the way, reflect something different (see Chapter 19).

18

Federal Government Securities

Probably the most secure investments of all are U.S. Treasury securities—Treasury Bills, Treasury Notes, and Treasury Bonds. These are the securities the U.S. Government uses to fund our Federal debt, and as long as there's a Federal government these are certain to be honored.

The essential difference among the three of them is maturity. The Bills come in maturities of up to one year; the Notes are for one to five years, and the Bonds are for twenty years and even longer. You can buy Treasury securities through your bank or securities broker or even directly from the Federal government through regular auctions that are reported in your newspaper. Realistically, it doesn't make much sense to bid at auction when the fee for acquisition of, say, a $10,000 Treasury Bill from your bank is usually around $25.

Things get trickier, though, when you move on to Federal government agency issues like Ginnie Maes. In periods of low interest especially, Ginnie Mae ads sound enticing: Government insured, liquid, near 12% yields. What investor, contemplating the 7% yield in his money market account, wouldn't be interested? But, as usual where there are promises of high yield these days, there's a catch. In fact, with Ginnie Maes—so often hawked lately for their higher-than-money-market yields—there is more than one catch. That is not to say that Ginnie Maes are not a good investment for you; it is only to note that these government-backed securities are very complicated and often are misrepresented or misunderstood.

Basically, Ginnie Maes are $25,000-or-larger pieces of multimillion-dollar pools of long-term government-insured mortgages. Investment bankers work with the Government National Mortgage Association to create these pools. An investor who holds an actual Ginnie Mae has possession of a certificate that gives him a share in a specific mortgage pool. It is roughly comparable to a long-term bond but with some key differences. His Ginnie Mae investment is secured by Veterans Administration (VA) and Federal Housing Administration (FHA) mortgages, which in turn are insured by the Federal government.

The price and yield quotations for Ginnie Maes that you see in your daily newspaper on the government bond pages—identified as GNMA Issues—refer to certificates from these pools. The quoted interest rate is the face amount, or interest rate that appears on the Ginnie Mae certificate. That is the rate you were promised if you bought the original certificate. The yield quoted in the newspaper is the current return, were you now to purchase one of these certificates at the current market price in the secondary market. Like all long-term bonds the price of the underlying security drops as outside interest rates rise and increases as rates fall. That means that if you sell your Ginnie Mae when interest rates generally are higher than they were when you bought it, you will receive an amount that is proportionally lower than you paid; and if you sell when rates are lower, you receive proportionally more. When interest rates are relatively low and there is some expectation that they will rise over the next six months or so, buying any long-term bond is unattractive. In short, if you buy a Ginnie Mae when rates are low that has an advertised yield of 11.5%, a price decline could result from general interest rate increases that could substantially reduce your actual return were you forced to sell. To make matters worse, with a Ginnie Mae you might not even realize what had happened.

What makes Ginnie Maes even trickier than most long-term bonds is that the checks you receive along the way are not purely interest payments, as they would be with a Treasury Bond, for example. You are also getting pieces of your principal, or original investment, back as borrowers pay off mortgages—often before they are due. As a result, when you reach the maturity date, you already will have gotten everything back. There will be no return of your original investment as with most bonds because you already have received it in pieces. Even if you hold to maturity, you can't be 100% certain of getting the original projected return, since early repayment of high-interest mortgages in the portfolio can reduce the yield to below what was anticipated. Ginnie Maes do generally return slightly more than Treasury Bonds, however. On average they will pay you about one percentage point more. When twenty-year Treasury Bonds are yielding about 10%, Ginnie Maes of the same maturity are yielding you around 11%. One suspects the difference in yield is partly to compensate you for having to deal with the tricky nature and confusing dividends of Ginnie Maes and in recognition of the fact you may not collect the full amount because of early loan repayments.

In practice, many Ginnie Mae investors don't buy the real Ginnie Mae certificates. Instead these are repackaged and broken into smaller pieces for smaller investors. The repackaging is generally done by large securities brokerage firms, who buy Ginnie Maes and break them into units that sell for $1000 or so. These unit investment trusts and the resulting shares behave just like Ginnie Maes, but of course you must pay an additional charge for the repackaging, and the Ginnie Maes become the security backing the units. These units also can be resold and behave much like the actual Ginnie Mae certificates in the resale, or secondary, market.

Besides the certificates and units a third alternative for investing in Ginnie Maes is to buy shares in a Ginnie Mae mutual fund through a mutual fund switching family. There are several advantages to this option. The primary one is that you can switch your money out of the fund instantly if the asset value of the shares starts to drop, and you can get daily quotes on the actual yield of the fund each day. In addition, the fund reinvests all the payments of interest and principal to save you that aggravation. The biggest disadvantage is that Ginnie Mae mutual fund shares never mature, and thus their asset value rises and falls against interest rates. Another big problem, both with the funds and unit trusts, is that many so-called Ginnie Mae funds really invest in a wide range of mortgage securities, some not backed by the Federal government. Read the fine print closely; there may be a reason one Ginnie Mae fund promises a higher yield than another—namely higher risk.

There are other government agency securities, but Ginnie Maes are the most popular with individual investors. They aren't the highest yielding products of the bond-issuing agencies, however. That honor goes to the little-known Small Business Administration (SBA), which guarantees and repackages its business loans for private investors. Don't spend time trying to figure out how to buy these SBA bonds unless you are ready to shell out big and peculiar amounts like $156,985. In fact, some SBAs do make their way into government agency fund packages and boost the returns of those funds.

19

Corporate Bonds and Preferred Stock

Corporate bonds are the way many companies borrow money. They issue bonds or debentures that pay interest in the form of dividends and when these debentures mature—in say ten years—they repay the original investment. You can buy a bond when it is issued, or you can go into the secondary market and buy one that was previously issued. Prices of many corporate bonds trading in the secondary market are quoted daily on the big stock exchanges just like stocks.

Corporate bonds are rated on the scales given at the end of Chapter 16. Depending on the amount of risk that the rating agency believes there is in a bond issue, it might be rated anywhere from AAA (by Standard and Poor's scale) for extremely strong to D, a rating that suggests probable trouble and an issuer that can't cover his dividend payments. In general, corporate bonds pay higher interest than government or government agency bonds because there is a bit more risk. There is no reason, however, why a little investor shouldn't put bonds rated, say, A into his Individual Retirement Account. This is the third-strongest rating, and the corporate bonds in this category are considered basically "strong," while in general having the advantage of paying ¾ percentage points more than AAA-rated corporates or government agency securities like Ginnie Maes.

If you decide to go lower than A ratings to try for a better return on your bonds, you should invest through bond mutual funds. Many mutual fund management companies offer corporate bonds in several speculative, higher-risk rating categories. The highest risk of all is the category known as "junk bonds," which generally includes bonds rating BBB (Standard & Poor's) or Baa (Moody's) and lower. Such bonds are a bit risky under any condition, but become less so through a diversified high-risk mutual fund.

One of the types of bonds you may encounter is the *convertible bond*. Convertibles are debentures that work like ordinary bonds but also offer some sort of alternative. For example, a particular issue might be convertible at the request of a bondholder into shares of the issuing company's stock. Since stock and bond prices tend to go up or down under roughly the same market conditions, convertibles—at any given time—can move in market price either with interest rate movements or stock market movements. In general, convertibles are less attractive for your IRA than ordinary bonds because part of their value comes from the equity conversion that they offer.

Terms of the conversions vary widely and individual investors should stay away from convertible bonds unless they get expert advice.

Similarly, *preferred stocks* are not as attractive for IRAs as ordinary bonds, even though preferred stocks behave in the market place more like bonds than stocks. They pay a large dividend and have a yield like bonds. They are called preferred because companies promise to pay dividends on them before paying dividends to ordinary shareholders.

The main reason preferred stocks are unattractive for individual investors—inside or outside their IRA—is that corporations get an 85% tax break on interest income from preferreds while individual investors do not. As a result of that tax break, yields tend to be much lower than for comparable bonds with no tax advantages for corporations.

20

Tax-Exempt Securities

This is the one type of interest-bearing security you will never want to put into your IRA, since the income it generates is already tax-exempt and as a result it pays interest at a lower rate than taxable securities.

With the latest round of tax reform there will be just one kind of tax-exempt security—municipal bonds. In prior years the municipalities could extend their tax protection to others—for example, the developer of a large shopping mall in the municipality—through redevelopment agency bonds secured by a portion of the property taxes. No more—although such bonds that already exist will probably retain their tax exemption.

Of course, tax-exempt securities would be foolish in your Individual Retirement Account. But outside your IRA, where you have no tax protection, municipals can be a big tax saver, even though there will be a bit less advantage to tax-exempts with lower-bracket taxes. In addition, state and municipal bonds are tax-exempt for residents of the issuing state and city.

Here's a look at some yields for municipals and comparable levels of yield that would be necessary in non-tax-exempt bonds to get the same after-tax return. (Bond yields, by the way, are the total return from a bond considering interest compounding and any difference between the original price of the bond and the price you would have to pay for the same bond in the current interest-rate market. Yield is the return—including dividends based on any change in value—you get if you buy it now; rate is what the issuer actually pays in dividends or coupons to its bondholders.)

As the table below demonstrates, if you are in the 35% tax bracket, it makes little sense to buy a municipal bond yielding 6% if a taxable bond of comparable quality yields 10%. In that case you will be better off after taxes if you buy the taxable security and pay the taxes. In recent years, however, tax-exempts have returned, on average, more than 80% of the yields of comparable taxables, making them a bit of a bargain.

Rating agencies put municipal bonds into roughly the same grades as commercial bonds, and the list, by the way, is at the end of Chapter 16. You should only buy them in grades A or better unless you decide to invest through a municipal bond fund or unit trust. As a result, they are only realistic choices if you would otherwise put your money into taxable bonds of comparable rating.

Buying minicipals can be tricky. The rules are quite different from those that apply in buying other bonds or stocks. Municipals trade over-the-counter—none are traded on exchanges—and consequently, different firms can quote you different prices on the same bond. The best way to buy municipals, if you opt to buy the securities directly rather than through funds or trusts, is to buy them from regional brokerage houses in your area, and it pays to deal with at least two so you can regularly compare prices and commissions.

COMPARABLE YIELDS FOR TAXABLE SECURITIES

Tax bracket	Yields for municipals					
	5%	6%	7%	8%	9%	10%
50%	10%	12%	14%	16%	18%	20%
35%	8%	9.5%	11%	12.5%	14%	15.5%

WAYS TO EARN INTEREST

In buying municipals you should be aware that the commission often is buried in the spread between the bid and asked prices of these bonds, which are quoted much like over-the-counter stock prices. (See Chapter 28 for an explanation of OTC spreads and quotes.) In general, the narrower the spread the better, since while you'll be buying at the asked price you will only be able to sell at the lower bid price. Some cynical bond customers say they always ask the broker for bid quotes first, as if they intended to sell. The result can be a lower asked price, they suggest. The point is that when dealing with municipal bonds you should shop around and negotiate.

When you go shopping for your first municipals, ask the brokers to supply price lists with specific bonds in the grade that interests you—A, for example—in various maturities. You should be sure to get the actual dollar price per bond as well as the yield to maturity.

Municipal bonds, by the way, are not tax-exempt for everyone. If you have margin accounts or have otherwise borrowed to buy these or any other securities (including the borrowing or letter of credit provisions in many tax-shelter limited partnerships), the IRS may disallow your tax exemption for municipals. You also may not get to deduct the interest if you use the bonds as collateral for a loan. On the other hand, you can get additional tax benefits from your municipals if the prices have fallen since you bought them. You can sell your municipals, taking a capital loss that you can use to offset any capital gains in your investment portfolio. Then you can use the money to buy more municipals with roughly the same yields, continuing your tax-exempt income stream uninterrupted.

21

Accumulation Bonds: Zeros and U.S. Savings Bonds

ZERO-COUPON BONDS

A postcard in your mailbox makes a magical promise: "Be a millionaire! Invest just $2000 a year and retire on more than a million dollars." You call the phone number and discover something called a zero-coupon bond. It builds up value like a U.S. Government Savings Bond but faster since it pays more interest. And although the interest in a zero doesn't accumulate tax free—unlike a government savings bond—within your IRA it has that effect, since you don't pay taxes on profits that are earned until you cash out.

For every $350 you invest in a zero-coupon bond today, you will get back $1000 in ten years. At least that will be your return if you get a compounded rate of roughly 11%. Investing $2000 a year at this rate for nearly forty years you should hit the $1 million mark. If you buy your zero when rates are lower, you will get less; on the other hand if you buy when rates are higher, you will get more.

Zeros must be magic, you figure. They can turn an $80,000 investment into a million dollars. But the real magic is in compounded interest—the money that builds up as you get back interest on your interest. The tables following the introduction (see p. 8) show how much and how fast your money will grow over different periods of time and at different rates. By calculating how much you will need at retirement—adjusting for inflation—and how long you have to accumulate that sum, you can figure out how much interest you must receive along the way.

Zero-coupon bonds aren't the only way to get such compounded interest in your IRA; money market accounts compound interest, although most pay much lower rates of interest today than zeros. And you can get the same effect by investing in a long-term-bond mutual fund that will reinvest your dividend payments for you. The primary advantages of these vehicles over ordinary long-term bonds is that they tend to pay slightly higher interest, and you don't have to remember to reinvest your dividend payments along the way. Beyond that, since dividend checks from ordinary long-term bonds can come in odd amounts—such as $132.76—steady and immediate reinvestment can be cumbersome if not impossible. And zeros backed by Treasury securities can be bought in $500 and smaller pieces, while you would need to invest $5000 to buy an actual Treasury Note.

Zero-coupon bonds are so named because they have no interest rate coupons or dividend payouts. Instead, the potential interest accumulates and is paid out in one balloon when the bond matures. If you held zeros outside your IRA, you would have to pay taxes on the theoretical interest buildup, even though you wouldn't actually collect it until the bond matures. Inside your IRA the interest buildup is protected from taxes, and thus the phantom interest is not a problem. In short, it would be foolish to buy zeros outside your IRA or Keogh.

Zeros usually offer perhaps half a percentage point more in interest than non-zeros of comparable quality. Today there are corporate zeros of every quality from top-rated AAAs to so-called junk bonds rated B and lower.

In addition there are the original and most popular zeros, which are backed by U.S. government Treasury securities. These include CATS (Certificates of Accrual on Treasury Securities), which are packaged for other brokers by Salomon Brothers, and TIGRS (Treasury Investment Growth Receipts) from Merrill Lynch. Active secondary markets now exist where you can resell these securities.

The problem with zeros is that they make better investments at some times than others. And if interest rates are low, or beginning to rise, it's no time to buy a zero—and it may in fact be a good time to sell old high-yielding zeros to take advantage of big increases in market price. The market price swings in zeros sold in the secondary markets have proved to be even sharper than for ordinary bonds. When interest rates are low you might want to resist buying zero-coupon bonds, even if you intend to hold on to maturity. That's because you may collect more interest in fewer years at a substantially higher rate if you park your money temporarily in a money market account than if you lock into a zero for 20 years at, say, 9%.

U.S. GOVERNMENT SAVINGS BONDS

You know how your Individual Retirement Account works—interest is allowed to compound tax-free until you are ready to withdraw the money. What you may not know is that there is a way to collect compounded interest tax-free outside your IRA—the common U.S. Government Savings Bond.

The Series EE government savings bond—the sort that is often bought by workers through payroll deduction—accumulates interest in the same way as zero-coupon bonds. But unlike zeros, which must be held inside your IRA to compound tax-free, the accumulating interest on EE bonds is tax-free wherever you hold them. As a result it would be foolish to put Savings Bonds in your IRA.

Outside your IRA these tax-protected bonds may make good sense in some cases. While interest paid on savings bonds is still lower than other bonds—today it's pegged to 85% of the five-year Treasury Note—these securities build up tax-free interest, making the ultimate earnings—particularly if the bonds are owned and eventually cashed in by someone in a low-tax bracket—potentially higher than from taxable Treasury and other securities. For example, if you buy a Series EE bond for your young child, the income would be taxed at his tax rate of the time of cashing—assuming he was no longer your dependent—which could be substantially lower than your own tax rate. Although the new tax laws will probably eliminate most tax sheltering that now can result from putting assets in the name of your child, Series EE Savings Bonds wouldn't be subject to your tax rate over the years while interest was accumulating, since they aren't subject to taxation until they are redeemed.

The tax protection of EE bonds is similar to IRA tax protection in that income earned over the life of the bond is taxable as income only when it is withdrawn. Unlike your IRA, however, there is no predetermined age at which you must begin to cash in ten-year EE bonds and take the profits—you get an automatic extension of up to forty years if you don't redeem at maturity. Thus you can cash in the bonds and start paying taxes when you want to—although the bonds stop earning interest when they mature.

If you redeem a mature bond even to buy another EE bond, you must pay taxes on the accumulated interest at that time. But a second series of savings bonds—Series HH—permits you to defer taxes even further. You can move from a mature Series EE into a Series HH without being taxed in the transfer and begin getting interest payments—the U.S. Treasury will send you checks—twice a year at the rate of at least 7.5% until these bonds mature ten years later. Of course, you must then pay taxes on the interest, but none of the earnings from U.S. savings bonds are ever subject to state or local taxes.

In years past Series E and EE bonds payed dividends on a fixed low scale that gradually rose to 7%; these older bonds still pay by that scale. That permitted you to buy a bond with a face amount of, say, $50 for $25. You paid $25 and redeemed your bond 11 years later for $50. The EE bonds you buy today look similar, but in fact give you a better deal since they are pegged to yield 85% of the average return on five-year Treasury Notes. Thus you may pay $25 for an EE bond with a face amount of $50, but when you go to cash in ten years later you may get more than $50. For example, the semiannual yield of Series EEs paid by the Treasury in December 1985 was 8.36%, down from 10.94% a year earlier but still better than the 7.5% floor on today's bonds held longer than five years. To find out what the Treasury is currently paying on EE bonds you can call your local Federal Reserve branch—in New York the phone number is 212-791-5965—and get a recording that will give you the current semi-annual interest rate and other news about your bonds.

You can buy Series EE bonds in small bites with face amounts like $50 (cost-$25), $75, or $100, as well as big $10,000 ones. This means you can invest in small pieces along the way and cash in the same small ways, only paying taxes as you need to.

But savings bonds aren't apt to replace tax-exempt municipal securities in the portfolios of America's wealthy. The maximum amount of Series EE bonds you can buy in a year is $15,000 (issue price) and your annual limit for Series HH ones is $20,000 (face amount), which is all you could roll over in one year.

There are a few disadvantages to savings bonds. For one thing, you can't sell them to someone else; you can only redeem them. And you can lose interest when you redeem, although you are guaranteed a return of at least

WAYS TO EARN INTEREST

7.5% if you redeem after five years. If you trade in before your five years are up, you will be paid interest on a graduated scale going from 5% to 7%. Other drawbacks are that you can't use them as security for a loan, that your brokerage house can't hold them for you in a street name as it does other securities, and that you probably can't even buy them from your broker. You buy them, by the way, at most banks, where you often can also redeem them if the bank is an authorized paying agent for the U.S. Treasury. You can also redeem them at any branch of the Federal Reserve Bank. If you have any problems, contact the Bureau of Public Debt, Securities Transactions Branch, Washington D.C. 20266, or the local Federal Reserve branch.

22

Unit Trusts and Bond Mutual Funds

In the growing competition for your investment dollar the big financial institutions are leaving no stone unturned. Take super-risky securities like junk bonds that once were the province of specialized institutional traders. Today you can buy, say, $1000 worth of a well-diversified junk bond mutual fund and the shares are substantially less risky—since all the issuing companies of bonds held by a fund aren't apt to default at one time—than if you had only acquired bonds from a single junk bond issuer.

So-called junk bonds, by the way, are simply bonds that are rated by the agencies as below "investment grade," generally Baa or lower. (See the end of Chapter 16 for a list of the ratings.) As a practical matter, few such bonds are defaulted in any one year—even during the Great Depression less than 3% of the outstanding bonds went into default. The point is that any real, identifiable risk of default is too much risk for most investors.

Where such high-risk securities are involved, or where an investment such as commercial paper only comes in giant $100,000-sized portions, ways have been devised to create big investment pools and then break them down into bite-sized portions for little investors. The two main vehicles are mutual funds and unit trusts.

WAYS TO EARN INTEREST

UNIT TRUSTS

In unit trusts an investment sponsor—often a big brokerage house like Merrill Lynch—assembles the investments, which can be practically anything from municipal bonds to Ginnie Maes. The trust manager then offers shares with minimum purchases ranging from $500 to $2500. That's what you buy in a unit trust, a piece of the investment pool. When the investment pool throws off income you get a proportionate piece. Most unit trusts make monthly distributions to their holders, which differs from the semi-annual dividends paid on most bonds.

After a unit trust is set up, the securities are purchased and held by a trustee; no one manages the portfolio or buys and sells securities to profit from changes in market conditions. If the securities have a maturity date or ultimately self-liquidate like Ginnie Maes, the trust dissolves with the securities. To sell shares in a unit trust before it is liquidated, a shareholder can usually go through the original sponsor, who generally makes some sort of market in the shares. There is usually no competitive bidding—you have to take what you can get. In the case of unit trusts made up of municipal bonds, it is customary for the sponsor to pay a price based on the average bid price for the bonds in the portfolio. The bid price, as explained in Chapter 20, is usually quite a bit lower than the asked price that investors must pay for the bonds when they buy.

Unit trusts are an expensive way to buy securities, and not only because of the costly and limited resale market for the shares. There is usually a sales charge of 3% to 4% of your investment for the sponsor, equivalent to a "load" on mutual fund shares. No-load unit trusts do not exist. As a result it only makes sense to buy an investment this way when there are no alternatives and you intend to hold it to maturity.

An example of how unit funds may fill a need not

met by other institutions is in providing a market for the municipal bonds of smaller states. Tax-exempt mutual funds holding all-New York or all-California municipal bonds are widely available. Big states have enough investors interested in tax-exempt securities to make it worthwhile for mutual fund management companies to set up these funds, which also are exempt from state taxes when owned by shareholders who pay tax in that state. But investors in lower population states like Rhode Island miss out. This is where unit trusts enter the picture, since they can be set up for 100 or even fewer investors. Diversification in the portfolio means the bonds can be lower-grade and hence higher-yielding than the quality that should be bought in an individual issue, which means that even the 3% to 4% sales fee is almost offset, and that the investor who can save on state tax may find it worth considering.

In practice, it makes no sense to buy shares in unit trusts or even mutual funds if the assembled securities are top-grade and available outside the fund in small units. An investor would fare as well to buy shares in several AAA-rated corporate bonds as he would in a mutual fund or unit trust made up of those bonds. In such cases the investor would just be paying extra sales costs, and in the case of mutual funds, extra management fees.

BOND MUTUAL FUNDS

Unlike unit trusts, mutual funds are managed, with investments being bought and sold in the fund as time goes by. Of course, you pay a fee for that management. Load funds—where you also pay a sales commission to get in—tend to charge lower management fees than no-load funds.

Bond mutual funds do pay dividends to their shareholders just like unit trusts or the actual issuers of the bonds. But the funds aren't self-liquidating. When you want to get out of a mutual fund, you get the asset value of your shares from your mutual fund's management company. And asset share values for most big mutual funds are quoted daily in the *Wall Street Journal* and some other daily newspapers. What's more, many mutual funds are part of telephone switching families; with a telephone call, your money can be moved instantly, at asset value, from one fund to another.

When an investment that interests you—for example municipal bonds issued in a big state like New York—is available both through mutual funds and unit trusts, pick the mutual fund unless it is important to you to hold to maturity. Not only will you pay less in fees if it is a no-load fund, but you have the advantage of management of the investments by a professional, who can pick and choose new investments, to maximize safety and yields.

PART IV

Some Case Studies

WHAT sounds right in theory is often difficult to achieve in actual practice. For this reason, three case studies are included here to demonstrate how first-time investors starting out with different needs and facing different market conditions, might apply the strategies outlined in Chapters 3–6.

Of the cases two represent people who start out with $5000 or more for their first real investments and one concerns a family who can barely come up with $1000.

It is important to remember that even if you are like the last-mentioned, low-level investor there are financial products available for you. Which does not mean that the big institutions will exactly fall all over themselves to get your $500 account, since it costs more for them to set it up than they will make from it in profits. In fact, if you have just $500 no legitimate salesman, paid on commission, is going to spend much time with you unless he expects to get a big chunk of your money, and that's a salesman you will want to avoid.

But it is possible to find $500 mini-Certificates of Deposit at some savings banks and commercial banks. These work just like ordinary CDs but generally pay more interest than money market accounts if you are willing to commit your money for between one year and five years.

Lots of mutual fund management companies will permit you to open an account and invest in one of their funds with a minimum of $1000. Some, these days, have dropped that to $500 or even $250, particularly if you are setting up an IRA. Brokerage houses also offer unit trusts, shares of Ginnie Maes and other securities that once could only be bought in big denominations. Sometimes these shares, representing pieces of a high priced security, can be bought for less than $1000.

You can buy shares in one mutual fund through a management company or enter a family of funds with your $500 or $1000 investment that will permit you to switch with a telephone call from, for example, a fund made up of high-yield junk bonds to a money market fund.

You can even open an account with a full-service or discount stock broker, although this makes little sense, since trading fees will eat up much of your tiny investment. Typically brokers, including discount brokers, charge a minimum of $35 to buy or sell a stock for you, regardless of how small your order.

The first of the following examples concerns a young couple who are wringing $1000 out of their budget to initiate their first investment program this year. There is already $2000—or three month's salary—in a money market account for emergencies. They have plans to put aside at least $1000 a year over the next 14 years, possibly in IRAs. Their hope is to accumulate $40,000 to educate their two children.

23
Case Study One: Saving for College on $1000 a Year

The Morgans are a married couple in their late twenties. They have two growing children whom they hope to send to college, starting about fifteen years from now.

The investment environment, for purposes of this example, is as follows: Interest rates are currently at a low level, but are generally expected to start rising in the next few months. The stock market is breaking records and share prices are generally higher than they have been in years.

So far as the Morgans' investment goals are concerned, they expect to get started with just $1000 this year and plan to put aside $1000 or more each year for the next fourteen years. They figure it will take about $40,000 to educate their two children in public colleges fifteen years from now, taking into consideration a minimal inflation factor. In short, they want to find a way to turn those fifteen years of saving $1000 a year into at least $40,000 after taxes fifteen years from now. The tables at the end of the book's introduction show that the Morgans would need to get an annual return on their money, after taxes, of at least 12% to accomplish their goal.

The maximum amount that could be earned from the most suitable investments, based on the criteria in Chapter 3, would not pay interest at that rate in a period of low rates, either before or after taxes. Thus, the Morgans have a problem.

Today the tax law still allows parents to give gifts to their children of up to $10,000 a year, tax-free, in an account under the child's name. But that provision will be eliminated under the new tax law, and families with children headed for college will have problems similar to the Morgans'. It is unlikely that the Morgans this year can come up with more than $1000, thus the Clifford Trust route is out even if existing trusts continue to be legal under the new law.

They could probably invest in long-term Federal and top-grade commercial bonds or the money market—collecting returns of up to, say, 10% as long as they bought top-grade bonds that would mature exactly when they were needed. (That way their return wouldn't be reduced by any decline in market price along the way—they'd simply collect and reinvest the dividends or purchase zero-coupon bonds, which return all of the interest when they mature.)

The problem here is that even before taxes they are short of their 12% goal, and they would have to pay taxes on the interest they earned, cutting the return by 25%, even in a middle tax bracket. Thus, they would actually be investing at a rate of about 7.5% a year and come out some $10,000 short of their goal—a dilemma that could leave them with a choice between sending their children to two-year junior colleges or getting a second mortgage on their house.

One alternative would be to use their IRAs to accumulate the money tax-free for fifteen years. Even after deducting the 10% penalty on the withdrawn money and also paying income taxes on it, this strategy can increase the yield if the money is held long enough in an IRA. At 10% in a 25% bracket it would take six years (see the table in the Introduction) to hit the break-even point after the penalty. That, however, would still fall short of the mark.

Although for some people U.S. Government Savings Bonds are useful for accumulating tax-free dollars for education (see Chapter 21), for the Morgan's these supersafe bonds wouldn't generate enough interest—in times of low rates they can return as little as 7.5%—and the ten-year life of the savings bonds makes them the wrong maturity for the Morgans.

Their best bet would appear to be the Pick-a-rate strategy outlined in Chapter 5 and a 13% target rate. In the current year they would have to invest in something speculative like a junk bond mutual fund to stand a chance of getting that 13% yield. If they were lucky in escaping defaults in the portfolio, and their junk bond fund earned their target rate of 13%, they could expect a net yield of about 10% after adjusting for taxes at the 25% rate. As interest rates rose and higher quality bonds or shares in higher quality bond funds were available at 13%, the Morgans could invest some of their college money more conservatively.

If the Morgans then put these investments in their IRA, using the prior strategy, they would break even in five years, permitting them to get full benefit of the tax-free compounding for the remaining ten years. By putting the college funds in their IRA and using the Pick-a-rate strategy with a high target rate, the Morgans at least have a chance of reaching their $40,000 goal.

24
Case Study Two: Retirement Coming Up and Unprepared

The Meyers are a middle-aged couple who, after a lifetime of raising and educating their family, realize retirement is only fifteen or so years away. Until now the couple has had little time or money for investment; now it's a necessity. With family-raising expenses out of the way, these first-time investors have about $5000 to invest each year. But their investment criteria, as outlined in Chapter 4, should include high appreciation in their portfolio, since they are such late starters.

Let's give the Meyers a rather favorable investment environment: Interest rates have been high for some time but have just begun to fall. Which makes it an excellent time to go into the stock market, and Blue Chip stocks meet the Meyers' criteria. It also is a very good time to lock into long-term bonds.

One feasible investment for the Meyers would be to buy mutual fund shares making monthly purchases through a management company that offers a family of mutual funds with switching privileges. They can select a mutual fund composed of Blue Chip stocks or an index fund, which would be right for the prevailing market conditions described—with stock prices very low and about to turn up and Blue Chips probably the first to move. A list of the Blue Chips making up the Dow Jones Industrial Average appears in Chapter 27.

In a practical sense, the Meyers could probably invest directly in such stocks—through a discount broker—more cheaply than through a mutual fund, where they would be paying to have their money managed. The idea would be for them to buy and hold onto their stocks until interest rates had reached a low point and once again threatened to rise. Stock prices fall at such times and the Meyers would then have to move their money elsewhere to avoid losses.

Since the couple expects to have in excess of $5000 to invest in each of the next fifteen years, it would be a good idea to sock away the allowable maximum—$4000 a year—in an IRA. That leaves them with $1000 a year for stock purchases—which should be outside the IRA in case of losses and because profits from price increases could be taxed at the favorable long-term capital gains rate. Inside the IRA the couple can invest in high-quality bonds. With the prevailing market conditions they should be able to obtain yields of 12% or more.

If rates were low when they were ready to invest, it would be feasible for them to buy the bonds in the secondary market so they could stagger maturities—having some maturing in fifteen years, some in sixteen years, and so forth. That would protect the couple against drops in price when the bonds have to be sold to meet the government's withdrawal requirements.

It is unlikely that this precaution would be necessary if the Meyers bought high-rated top-quality bonds at the high rates that would apply under the market conditions described and the Meyers should probably buy the longest maturities available to keep generating income in the IRAs long after their retirement has begun. When the time comes to sell them—because of the high rates—it probably can be done at a profit.

25

Case Study Three: Single, Flush and Greedy

Miss Miller is single and earning enough money so that she can begin investing for future luxuries. Until now she's set aside money in annual IRAs for retirement—mostly in bank Certificates of Deposit. Now she's ready to try to make money.

With visions of a Park Avenue apartment, a Mercedes, a sable coat, and a thirty-five-foot sailboat, she's willing to take big risks in hope of reaping a reward.

Since she's so greedy, let's give her less than favorable market conditions: Let's say interest rates have been very low for three or four months with no promise of rising any time soon.

Some of the investment possibilities offered that she should *not* consider are the boiler room pitches for 50% returns on diamonds or the high pressure salesmen claiming they'll triple her money in three months. Nor is this really a time for her to consider tax shelter partnerships—it's too early for her to plan for the shelter of profits yet to come.

One possible way she can get started is with a mutual fund family that permits telephone switching. Many funds can give her choices like gold funds, energy funds, and even options funds. The market conditions she is operating in are best for little over-the-counter stocks and growth stock funds that specialize in small, speculative issues.

A margin account with a brokerage house would increase her prospect of big profits, while also increasing the risk, of course (see Chapter 13).

The prevailing market conditions aren't favorable for gold funds, stock options (either puts or calls), or investment in most commodities, which are three of the best high-risk, high-reward investments under the right conditions. Commodities investments and stock options are best when interest rates and markets prices are moving sharply up or down. Gold is best when interest rates are rising and high.

A more timely way for her to speculate might be to get into armchair arbitrage and buy stocks that are likely takeover candidates (as explained in Chapter 30). She might even do some of this in her IRA as a hedge to her current all-CD IRA portfolio. The over-the-counter stock market is another possibility for her, if she's willing to spend the necessary time and effort on original research.

She might even do some in-and-out stock trading in her IRA, with the tax shelter protecting her from the 50% short-term capital gains on the profits.

PART V

Playing the Stock Market

You may have turned to this section on the stock market from curiosity. The introduction suggested that even novice investors could beat most professionals in the stock market just by buying shares in a big mutual fund that mirrors one of the big stockmarket indexes like the Standard & Poor's 500. The index is made up of the 500 biggest stocks monitored by Standard & Poor's (S & P), a financial data-publishing company, and the performance of this group of stocks consistently exceeds the average of stockmarket mutual funds so that an increasing number of pension funds and other institutional investors have given up attempts to beat the market in disgust and moved their assets into index funds.

If a novice investor intends to put no effort at all into his stock selections, he would probably do better buying shares of index mutual funds than listening to advice of a professional stockbroker. But with some effort it is possible to outperform the indexes. Information collected by Goldman Sachs & Company, the securities firm, showed four ways you could have outpaced the S & P 500 index for the six years through 1984. Their strategies involved using the following:

Small company stocks. Little companies with low market capital—that's their number of shares times their share price—consistently outperform larger companies. Goldman Sachs data showed stock prices of the smallest 100 of the S & P 500 stocks climbed some 33% faster than the average of all 500. Little companies in the over-the-counter (OTC) market grew even faster than that. While it's hard work discovering and watching stocks of the smallest companies, it is well worth the effort (see Chapter 28).

High dividend stocks. These stocks grew 22% faster in price than the index, the six-year study found. An investor can do particularly well in these stocks if he buys them when stock prices are low, which is also when interest rates are the highest.

Stocks with low price earnings ratios (P/E) and stocks with high cash value per share. Stocks in these categories are frequently the ones that become takeover candidates, as is described in Chapter 30 on Armchair Arbitrage. Not surprisingly, these were the other two ways Goldman Sachs found to beat the index average. Since the potential for capital losses is less when a stock is selling at a low P/E or at a high cash value per share, these strategies might even make sense inside your IRA. A particularly good time to buy such stocks is when interest rates are low, even though general stock prices tend to be high at such times.

Unless you play the indexes or narrow down the field in the ways just described, there are no shortcuts in the stock market. Hot tips—particularly from your stockbroker—are a one-way ticket to disaster. (See Chapter 15 for advice on how to get restitution when things go amiss.) The little investor's best bet—if he's willing to work—is among undiscovered stocks in the over-the-counter market. But that means lots of do-it-yourself research, since the information you want isn't available from brokerage firm research departments.

As for investing in exchange-listed stocks you could select four or five at random from the thirty Blue Chip issues that make up the Dow Jones Industrial Average (see Chapter 27 for the list). Beyond that you should take advantage of the research departments of the big full-service brokerage houses that spend millions of dollars scrutinizing these companies. An individual can't compete with this research. But even if you use professional advice, you should not venture into exchange-listed common stocks without backgrounding yourself by reading stockmarket investment books like Benjamin Graham's, *The Intelligent Investor*, a classic, and subscribing to a financial daily newspaper and at least two sophisticated investment periodicals like *Forbes Magazine* and *Barron's*.

All stockmarket investments are a gamble—your principal is at risk. For big-time gamblers there is the options market, where you can risk all of your principal at once in the hope of making big profits. You can even play the index-fund odds in the options market. How? By continuously buying future calls on the Standard & Poor's 500 or any other general market index at strike prices equal to the current level of the index, which is reported daily in the *Wall Street Journal*. (For a look at how index options work, see Chapter 32.)

While such an options strategy may be ill-advised for your IRA, you might try purchasing the index options inside your IRA when interest rates are falling sharply or are particularly low, since that's when you're most likely to make a profit. You may be hard pressed to find an IRA custodian who will let you do this, however. When interest rates start to rise or continue at high levels you must continue buying calls if you're faithful to the strategy. At that point though you might want to buy the calls outside your IRA so that you can use your capital losses to write off against capital gains. (See Chapter 32 for tax rules affecting options.)

26

Scams and Warnings

There are, quite simply, hundreds of con men and just plain high-pressure salesmen out there hoping to lay their hands on your investment dollars. To be sure, the scammers are less interested in your $1000 than in $100,000 in the hands of a similarly inexperienced investor. But in the last few years boiler rooms have come to the stockbrokering business to engage in mass marketing of sometimes questionable stocks even to the smallest investor with just a few hundred dollars in his pockets. A number of the salesmen in these boiler rooms are holdovers from the commodities boiler rooms of the late 1970s and their telephone sales tactics are the same: "Mr. Jones, I honestly think you're afraid to make money... The big boys know you have to spend money to make money... The price just went up again while you were talking... Look, I'm putting in your order, what's the name of your bank?"

Most commonly these tactics are used to push obscure stocks in the over-the-counter market and hot new stock issues many of which are brought out at inflated prices or issued for companies that have almost nothing to sell. For example, Universal Shark and Marine came out a few years ago with total assets of four Panamanian shark fishing boats. It soon folded after it discovered Panamanian fishermen were less than willing workers. Dennings Mobile Robotics went public with an idea for a robot (no patent had been applied for) and a drawing in the prospectus that might or might not look like the actual robot if it were ever completed.

With hot little stocks pushed by boiler room salesmen, the broker can virtually control market prices if he so desires, especially when only a few brokers make markets in such stocks. The result: prices quoted for the stock rise sharply while the salesmen are putting more and more new investors into the issue. When they've run through the pack, the stock price collapses and you're left holding the bag.

Here are a few tips to help keep you away from the scammers:

Deal with established brokers. It helps if the brokerage house or financial advisor recommending the stock has been around long enough to get listed in the telephone book.

Buy stocks, don't get sold. And if you feel uncomfortable after you've bought, sell. Often the enthusiasm of your salesman relates more to his potential commissions that to profits for you. With some firms salesmen have to give up their commission if you decide to sell back a new issue in less than six months, so they're not about to advise you to sell.

Always ask for the 10-K filing from the Securities & Exchange Commission and the annual and quarterly reports of the company whose stock is being promoted. For new issues demand the prospectus. If the product or the management look shaky, or it there is no product or service, pass it up.

27

Exchange-Listed Stocks

Time was when the big Blue Chip stocks that traded on the New York Stock Exchange were considered a solid and growing piece of America. Children were given shares of General Motors or U.S. Steel that they kept to retirement, watching the value slowly climb year by year and the dividends mount in their savings accounts. No more.

When interest rates soared in the late 1970s, prices of the Blue Chips (nicknamed after the top-value poker chip) tumbled along with everything else, leaving both big and little investors adrift in their search for something solid to hold onto. Today, in big market rallies like the one that started in August 1982, the Blue Chips are the first to rise in value. That's why the Dow Jones industrial average—which is composed of thirty big NYSE Blue Chips in a cross-section of industries—often jumps sooner and at first higher than the broader market indexes like the Standard & Poor's 500 or the NYSE index of the 1500 or so stocks traded there.

If you want a simple way to get into the stock market before such a rally—when stock prices are low but interest rates have begun tumbling—you might buy, through a discount broker, a random selection of four or five of the varied and diversified Blue Chips that make up the Dow Jones Industrial Average. Here are the stocks that make it up:

Allied-Signal	Inter. Harvester
Aluminum Co.	Inter. Paper
Amerian Can	McDonald's
American Express	Merck
AT&T	Minnesota M&M
Bethlehem Steel	Owens-Illinois
Chevron	Philip Morris
DuPont	Procter & Gamble
Eastman Kodak	Sears Roebuck
Exxon	Texaco
General Electric	Union Carbide
General Motors	United Technology
Goodyear	U.S. Steel
Inco	Westinghouse El.
IBM	Woolworth

READING THE AVERAGES

At one time I wrote a daily column that tracked stock market activity. On any given day I would quote market experts explaining why the Dow Jones Industrial Average had dropped five points or risen ten a day earlier.

Such columns no doubt give readers a sense of security and order. The Dow may drop six points but the experts have the situation under control, explaining the problem as an adverse reaction to sudden unexpected growth in the money supply or hints that corporate earnings in the company quarter may be lower than anticipated. Readers might feel less secure if they knew that the writers of such columns get the same experts at the same time to explain why the market went up. The reason is that the market can suddenly reverse in the last hour of trading and market columnists—writing on a deadline that comes minutes after the 4:00 P.M. market close—must be prepared. Thus two stacks of opinion mount on the columnist's desk: one with expert explanations of why the market went down and a second with equally convincing reasons why it went up. What this means is that small day-to-day moves in the averages are basically meaningless, no better understood by the experts than by you. It is only when a trend is sustained over a period of weeks or months that the averages take on meaning and can be truly analyzed. The one exception is a huge one-day, or even one-hour, move in a wide variety of indexes. In such cases a reason can often be pinpointed.

Sudden and big movements in the Dow and other averages are far more common today than five years ago, as any regular reader of the financial pages has soon deduced. The reason is that today's traders for big institutions like banks and insurance companies have the authority to make instant buy or sell decisions. Five years ago such decisions were pondered by committee over days or even weeks. Today when traders for dozens of institutions all receive by computer the same information at the same time, six institutions can instantly decide to sell millions of dollars worth of stock at the same time—and bang, the Dow moves six points in a single hour. At one moment the herd may be thundering forward—seconds later everything reverses and they all move the other way.

How can a little investor avoid getting trampled? There are certain days when the market tends to be particularly volatile, and the small investor might try to avoid trading on those days. One such time is the third Friday of each month, which is the settlement day for option contracts. As institutional and other investors scurry to cover their options' positions, the underlying stocks often behave erratically. It also helps to understand the various market indexes—know what makes them move and what they actually reflect. You should be aware, for example, that any such particular index may have little to do with your particular stock portfolio. Let's take a look at several of them:

The Dow Jones Industrial Average (DJIA). This much-publicized index has been around since before the Depression when Dow Jones, publisher of the *Wall Street Journal*, put together a list of thirty industrial stocks which it felt were representative of the entire market. Each day at the close of the market a few quick calculations produced the DJIA and two other indexes based on twenty transportation stocks and fifteen utilities stocks. (Dow Jones also has a composite index that combines all three indexes, but it is rarely quoted.) If you should hold a diversified portfolio of Blue Chip stocks, the DJIA is probably a good indicator. All thirty of its currently listed stocks are among the largest traded on the New York Stock Exchange. But its reputation comes principally from its long history going back to when large public companies could be counted in the hundreds and to precomputer times before the prices of thousands of stocks could be averaged and calculated in seconds by computer.

The Standard & Poor's 500. The S & P—a subsidiary of McGraw-Hill Inc., publisher of *Business Week*—averages 500 issues instead of thirty, making it a broader measure than the Dow Jones Industrial Average.

The New York Stock Exchange Index. This is based on a composite of the 1500 or so issues that trade on the NYSE, which is the world's largest. The average includes the thirty monitored by Dow Jones and the 500 tracked by S & P along with 1000 smaller stocks, making the NYSE composite a much broader market index.

NASDAQ. The National Association of Securities Dealers automated quotation system—NASDAQ—reflects prices of more than 4100 issues traded in the over-the-counter market. This index does not overlap with

PLAYING THE STOCK MARKET

the prior three. It is the one to watch if you hold primarily over-the-counter stocks.

Wilshire 5000. This is the index to watch if your stock portfolio includes stock issues of all sizes. It includes everything from the largest to the smallest public companies, whether the stocks trade on an exchange or in the over-the-counter market.

Each of these indexes is quoted daily in financial newspapers. For each there is the daily average—say 1530 for the DJIA, 120.10 for the NYSE, etc.—and a percentage gain or loss for the day. You can compare activity in the various markets by comparing the percentage changes.

28

Over-the-Counter Stocks

There are many reasons to stay away from the tiny stocks that pepper the bottom of the over-the-counter market. For one thing, dealings in these stocks are less well policed than on the big stock exchanges. A few questionable brokers or market makers can easily control these little stocks—making prices go up or down to suit their own interests, which are often quite different from your own.

But in spite of the potential hazard there is one compelling reason to consider investment in small and obscure stocks. For it is here, among the smallest and least-known issues in the over-the-counter market that the little individual investor stands his best chance of making big profits—inside his IRA or out. Small and obscure companies do not command the interest of institutional investors and their big research departments, who rarely invest less than $500,000 at a clip. As a result there is less competition for the shares and prices of the small OTC stocks tend to be cheaper in terms of potential earnings and growth than stocks of larger companies. What's more, if and when the little companies grow big enough to attract institutional buyers in the future, the price of your shares will get an additional boost.

Over-the-counter stocks, by the way, are simply the collection of public stocks—some 11,000 of them—that aren't traded over any of the big stock exchanges. Some aren't traded on an exchange because they are too small or their stock is too tightly controlled by a single owner.

Others aren't traded on an exchange because they elect not to be, preferring the over-the-counter system of multiple market makers.

Prices of some of these issues are quoted daily in your newspaper through the National Association of Securities Dealers Automated Quotation System (NASDAQ), but those are primarily the larger OTC stocks. Substantially more issues are quoted daily among brokers through a private price list known as the Pink Sheets. And while prices of little OTC stocks to some degree follow trends among the big stocks, as measured by common indexes like the Dow Jones Industrial Average, in many ways these individual little issues have a life all their own. In short, they just don't follow the same rules as the big exchange-listed stocks. And one can often sift through and profitably play little OTC stocks, even when the general stock market is in a decline.

Marc Reinganum, an associate professor of finance at the University of Southern California, has spent several years comparing stockmarket performance of the smallest stocks with the larger ones in terms of total market capital. The result: small stocks—particularly the tiniest over-the-counter ones with market capital of less than $15 million when you add up the value of all their outstanding shares—consistently outperform large stocks as to percentage gains in price.

In good times, he has found, the little stocks way outperform the big ones. Unfortunately, their market prices fall more drastically in bad times than do prices of the big ones. A 10% drop in market prices overall can produce a 15% decline in many over-the-counter stock prices. But if you average changes in both good times and bad times, overall price appreciation for the small stocks is better than for the large ones. According to Reinganum, the biggest gains in prices of over-the-counter stocks regularly come in January. Frequently stockmarket prices of little OTC stocks hit a low point at the end of

December—when investors sell for tax reasons—then show roughly half their annual gains in January. In short, it makes sense to plan to buy the shares in late December when prices tend to drop. Consider it the annual after-Christmas sale.

PICKING WINNERS

Investing in obscure OTC stocks is far trickier than investing in larger stocks. For one thing, it is next to impossible to spot a certain winner among the littlest companies, even though on average these tiny stocks outperform big exchange-listed ones. Reinganum found that in a random portfolio of ten small over-the-counter stocks, on average two would drop sharply in price over a year's time, six would show little change in price, and two would leap in price. The net result, he found, was a sharp improvement in value of the ten-stock portfolio since those with big gains in price way outpaced the price collapses of the losers.

This suggests that a possible way to go into little OTC stocks is to pick enough, by random, to benefit from average performance. There is a good chance that you can benefit from the statistics if you invest in a portfolio of ten randomly selected OTC stocks, putting, say, $1000 in each. But beyond that, there are certain ways to improve your odds, remembering that OTC rules are quite different from those that benefit an investor playing with big Blue Chip stocks.

Extensive research is done by institutions like brokerage houses into large stocks that they consider good prospects for buying or selling or recommending to their customers. Research reports and buy and sell reports on these big issues are available from the big brokerage houses through stock market newsletters and computer data banks. However, by the time a little OTC stock is big enough to interest an institution or two, it's realized much of its early growth potential. In short, it has been discovered, and the accompanying runup in stock price that tends to accompany that discovery is in the past. It goes without saying that if a brokerage house salesman is calling you with tips on hot little over-the-counter growth stocks, the undiscovered profit potential is past, if it ever was there in the first place. In addition, there is often manipulation of little issues that are telephone-peddled to mass markets of investors.

DO-IT-YOURSELF EVALUATION

If you want your own undiscovered gems, you must find them yourself. That isn't easy if you are not a professional research analyst, but it is possible. If you are lazy, shopping in the tricky OTC market is not for you.

There are several newsletters that specialize in weeding out jewels among the small stocks. Most go first to big customers of the publishers, who also act, for a fee, as investment advisor or OTC fund manager to high-ticket customers. One newsletter that doesn't double as advisor-for-a-fee is the Value Line OTC Special Situation Service (711 Third Ave., NYC), which costs $300 a year. There are also mutual funds like T. Rowe Price's New Horizon's Fund which specialize in little stocks, although even these funds don't invest in many with market capital under $15 million.

GETTING STARTED

One approach is to look for little OTC companies that are geographically close enough for you to visit and to check out their products and services. If you live on Long Island, look for companies there; if you live in Brooklyn, look at Brooklyn-based companies.

When you find a good locally made product or service, follow up and see if a little OTC company is behind that product or service. What you need to do this is a copy of a corporate directory like Standard & Poor's three-volume *Register of Corporations* or Dun & Bradstreet's *Million Dollar Directory*, which has a geographic breakdown of companies. Both are available at local libraries. To get a list of all 11,000 or so companies that trade OTC you must obtain a copy of the daily Pink Sheets from your stockbroker; or buy one of several other publications put out by the National Quotation Bureau, Jersey City, N.J., which publishes the Pink Sheets. The company issues a *Weekly Price Digest* for $22 a month and a twice-a-year *National Stock Summary* for $65 a copy.

It is also possible to make a statistical sweep of 2400 of the OTC companies with a new computer software system just introduced by the Unlisted Market Service, (49 Glen Head Rd., Glen Head, N.Y. 11545.) The software service is available on-line through The Source, Quotron, or Newsnet. It also can be obtained on floppy disks for $695 plus $25 a month. Taken either way, an investor now can sift through the companies with dozens of parameters. For example, there are currently 434 OTC companies with price-earnings ratios under ten, says Scott Emrich, president of the company, and 176 are trading at prices that are less than cash per share.

Once you have identified, say, thirty potential OTC stocks, you are ready to begin your research. Information on these companies is in the Unlisted Market Service database; some also is available in computer data services offered by Media General and Standard & Poor's. From these sources and the corporate directories you should find the corporate address and write to each company requesting an annual report, quarterly reports (along with 10-K reports, 10-Q reports, and any prospectuses that have been filed with the Securities and Exchange Commission), and copies of any news releases issued by the company in the last year. Address your request to the company's chairman or president and identify yourself as a potential shareholder. Public companies, by law, must make their financial reports available to the public.

Now you are ready to dive into the figures: What sort of ratios and statistical guides are important in identifying little OTC stocks with big potential? They are different from the most significant ratios for analyzing larger issues. They include:

Price/Sales ratio. This may be the most important factor in spotting a hot little stock—even more important than price/earnings ratio, which is a standard guideline for selection of larger stocks. The price/sales ratio is a guide to future potential in a small, growing company which might not yet have oiled up assembly lines and taken other moves to improve productivity that would show up as earnings. Look for companies where revenue—or sales—per share is greater than the asked price of an OTC stock. This is derived by dividing total reported annual revenues by the number of common shares outstanding.

Spread. Prices of the smallest OTC stocks are generally quoted with both a bid price and an asked price. That's because in these infrequently traded issues OTC market makers get their profit from the spread between these two prices. The heavier the volume the less the market maker charges to hold onto the shares until he can find another buyer and the narrower the spread. For example, an OTC stock price might be quoted in the newspaper as 1¼ bid, 1¾ asked. That means if you want to buy shares, the market maker will sell them to your broker, who will then sell them to you for $1.75 a share, the asked price. If you want to sell shares of the same stock right back to the market maker—either directly or through your broker—you will only get $1.25 a share, the bid price. The spread compensates the market maker for the time he will probably have to hold the stock before he can find another buyer. And you will pay the usual commission to your broker.

On the biggest and most heavily traded OTC stocks the spread is narrow enough so that just a single last price is quoted for the issue, just as for stocks that are traded on the stock exchanges. Despite the apparent unfairness of the spread in OTC prices as compared with exchange-listed prices, you should look for wide spreads in your search for undiscovered OTC jewels because they suggest sluggishly traded stocks.

The spreads are one reason it doesn't make sense to trade in-and-out in the OTC market. You should plan to hold onto your ten-stock OTC portfolio at least a year. By that time, if your selected stocks were truly potential gems, not only will the stock prices have risen substantially but the spreads will have narrowed, permitting you to sell out at prices closer to the ones being paid by buyers.

A useful clue to undiscovered OTC stocks is the absence of big market makers—firms that are household words—like Merrill Lynch—or any of the mass marketing firms—like First Jersey Securities—that use the telephone and broadcasting to promote their services and the presence of more than three but less than eight smaller brokers that make markets in the stock. You will find the market makers listed by stock in the daily Pink Sheets or in the database or directory to 500 OTC companies from the Unlisted Market Service.

Perhaps the greatest analytical tool of all in zeroing in on OTC comers is good common sense; and here you may have some advantages over the professionals, who often tend to miss the forest while analyzing and charting out the individual trees. Here are some common-sense approaches assessing the potential of a small company and its stock:

Look for proprietary products. One of the beauties of the OTC market is that the anti-trust laws aren't as strictly interpreted as among big, public giants. All through the OTC market you will find single-line companies that dominate tiny and obscure areas of American industry— companies that have little or no domestic competition in their particular specialty. An example is the Thetford Corp., which dominates the American market for large and small portable toilets. Since such companies prefer not to wave red flags at the Justice Department, they are not likely to identify themselves as monopolies, but careful reading of competition sections is the annual 10-K reports they file with the SEC will guide you toward little companies that dominate little markets.

Look for growth industries. Obviously it is of no advantage to find a company with a near-monopoly in a dying industry. A company that dominates the buggy whip market cannot be expected to expand its market very much. Use common sense to decide whether there is any potential for growth or whether there is likely to be an onslaught of big corporate competitors once the emerging market takes hold.

Look for good management. Pay close attention to what the company's managers are saying and what they are doing. It is a good sign if management holds a big chunk of its own stock—say more than 15%—in a little OTC company. It means that the managers have a big incentive to see the stock does well. Look at the photographs of the company's officers in the front of the annual report. According to their own confidences, more than a few professional analysts have made a decision to sell shares that later plummeted in price because of a shifty look in the chairman's eye or an overly lush office in the background. Also read the biographies of the company's officers in the annual proxy material and in the 10-K. If their backgrounds appear inappropriate for their fields of endeavor—say, three ex-football pros with no prior real estate experience are running a land development company—discard that prospect and go on to your next.

Watch for signs of scams. Even professional investors from time to time get caught buying stocks in companies that turn up fraudulent. But your odds of surviving and thriving in the over-the-counter market improve markedly if you avoid any stock that sells for less than $1.00 a share or that has more than 1 million shares outstanding. That's a tip from Robert Flaherty, editor of the *OTC Review*, a monthly magazine from Review Publishing in Oreland, Pa.

Once you have picked them, you buy your OTC stocks much like any other stocks. Having done your own research and because some of the large full-service brokerage houses encourage their brokers to sell only shares on their own buy lists, you might want to consider a discount broker for these purchases. You can often buy the shares directly from the brokers who are market makers, but there is little incentive to do that in terms of commissions or executions.

29
How to Buy and Sell on News

In August 1975, the founder and chairman of Revlon, Inc.—Charles Revson—died. The following day the price of Revlon shares tumbled $2.25 to $67.75 a share. Logical? Yes. But consider this. When Charles Bluhdorn, founder and chairman of Gulf & Western Industries, Inc. died in February 1983, G & W shares climbed $2.25 to $20.25 a share. And by the end of the week the share price had moved up $6.75 a share, or 27%. What was the difference? Revlon was thriving under Revson. Gulf & Western, on the other hand, was not doing so well, and some investors saw Bluhdorn as a roadblock to possible takeover attempts.

In both cases the stocks prices reacted to news. This phenomenon is important to understand if you decide to play the stock market, in or out of your IRA. When the listed price of a stock suddenly jumps or falls $3 a share in one day, chances are good that some sort of news, or rumor of news, is behind the movement. To take advantage of this stock market effect as an investor you must first understand the mechanics of how news works to send stock prices up or down.

It is logical, but not always correct, to assume that good news will send stock prices up and bad news will send them down. Take the case of Apple Computer's earnings in the quarter ended in December 1984. Earnings leaped nearly eightfold to a record $46.1 million for the quarter, exceeding all expectations, according to Apple's chairman. But the stock immediately took a nosedive. Why? Because Apple's management had been predicting earnings of that magnitude for the December quarter, its stock price had already climbed in anticipation. That's called "discounting" in stockmarket lingo. The market discounted the potential leap in earnings by sending the stock price up in advance of the announcement.

If that were the only factor, Apple's stock price probably wouldn't have moved at all on the day of the announcement. Sometimes, however, a price will fall slightly when the good news is actually announced because speculators, who had already gotten into the market to take advantage of the anticipated announcement, sell out and take their gains. In the case of Apple, however, good news turned out to be bad news. Apple's chairman hinted that he expected the next quarter to be more difficult than the record first quarter. The stock tumbled in anticipation of second-quarter earnings. The hint of trouble in the second quarter rather than good earnings in the first quarter was the news that influenced interested investors and securities analysts. In short, the stock market is a very efficient mechanism that always discounts for expected good news and expected bad news. Only surprises send stock prices up or down—like the sudden deaths of Revson or Bluhdorn or the first hint of poor second-quarter earnings in the case of Apple.

News that affects stock prices can first appear in an exclusive newspaper or magazine story; it can come in a securities analyst's report; it can be released by a company to various news wires—such as Dow Jones or Reuters'—that are received directly by professional and some individual investors; or it can spread by word of mouth or over the telephone. It can be an official announcement disclosed by a company, a government agency or a court.

Or it can first appear as a rumor, in which case it should eventually prove true or false. If a widespread rumor turns out to be false, the stock will usually fall back to its original position. For example, a takeover rumor can send a stock price up several dollars a share, but it will tumble back to its original level if the company issues an outright denial or the potential acquirer moves to take over a different company. On the other hand, if the rumor proves true, the stock price will move up but only to the extent that the rumor was not widely spread or believed before it was corroborated.

In order to take advantage of news as it affects the stock market it is important to keep fully informed about any company with stocks that interest you, so you will know whether to credit or discount any news you hear about it. To help you in making the proper response, here is a look at how certain types of news often affect stock prices:

News that tends to send prices up:
- Takeover attempt proposed
- Big jump in future earnings projected
- Unexpected jump in reported earnings
- New contract that could increase future gross sales by 10% or more
- New product that could increase future sales by 10% or more
- Food and Drug Administration (FDA) approval of a drug that could make up more than 10% of future sales
- Court decision awarding damages to company that exceed those generally expected

News that tends to send stock prices down:
- Takeover attempt withdrawn; success of target company in fending off potential acquirer
- Forecast of lower earnings, slower growth
- Surprise report of lower earnings

- Legal or regulatory problems with a product that makes up more than 10% of sales
- Loss of contract that makes up more than 10% of sales
- Employees go out on strike

News that rarely has much effect on stock price:
- A new headquarters building is announced
- Management changes in an orderly succession
- Small new contract, minor new product or problem with a product that makes up a small part of sales
- Big announcement of public service project

30

Armchair Arbitrage

There are ways little investors can make money on hostile takeovers, possibly even in their IRA's, but once the stock price of the target company has gotten off the ground, you should do nothing but watch in fascination. Admittedly it's tempting to try and get in on the action when the stock price of the target company leaps one day to $25, the next day to $30, and on to $35 as a new company enters the ring amidst rumors it is about to offer $40.

There are three good reasons you should restrain yourself. First, once the price of a stock has lifted off its natural base in a hostile takeover situation—which it does quite rapidly in the first day or even the first hour after the offer—the way back down is farther and harder than the potential way up. Say the above stock was trading around $15 a share when the rumors started and shot up in several days to $25 a share. It might go to $30 a share if the rumors are true, but even then, some hitch could arise causing potential problems in the merger and the stock price could tumble overnight back to the original $15 or less. Suddenly you've lost half your investment.

Sometimes potential takeovers by even solid and solvent companies don't happen. In 1979 American Express went after McGraw-Hill, the publisher of *Business Week* and owner of Standard & Poor's. McGraw-Hill fired back with nasty charges in newspaper advertisements and elsewhere. American Express, concerned about its public image, withdrew and the price of McGraw-Hill's stock plunged by nearly one-third. McGraw-Hill's counter-attack was so effective no one else has ever tried to raid it.

Beyond that, the real players in takeovers are the risk arbitragers, who know lots of things you don't know. For them it's a calculated risk—for you it's Russian roulette. Which is the second reason you should keep out of the way once the real action starts.

Consider this. In 1977 I was a reporter for the *Wall Street Journal*, sitting in a courtroom in Hartford, Connecticut, listening to a hearing about whether or not Norton Simon would be allowed to buy Avis, the rent-a-car company, which was fighting the takeover. With Avis's court-appointed trustee in mid-sentence it was suddenly clear to me that by the time he finished the sentence the potential hostile takeover would be approved. *Wall Street Journal* reporters file news bulletins on the Dow Jones News Wire in competition with reporters for another news service, Reuters. Unsure whether Reuters had anyone in the out-of-the-way courtroom but well aware there was only one public telephone on the courthouse floor, I leaped out of my seat in the front row and dashed for the door at the back of the courtroom. A split-second later nearly everyone in the courtroom—at least thirty well-groomed men in conservative business suits—followed at a fast clip.

In this story I reached the phone first—and the public was first to learn of the decision over the Dow Jones wire while thirty angry, even hostile, arbitrage employees paced back and forth outside the phone booth. Had anyone of them reached the phone first, millions of dollars of Avis stock could quickly have been bought by the arbitrager who got the call before anyone else knew what was happening. This was my first taste of risk arbitrage, a multimillion dollar world where small scraps of information are worth millions and sometimes hundreds of millions of dollars. With this much money on the line no expense is spared in the search for information. Couple that with the fact that the chairman of a company is much more likely to accept a telephone call from an arbitrager holding 17% of the stock of his company than he is your call, and you begin to get the picture. The chairman doesn't have to give the arbitrager inside information, like "now we're going to sue the bastards in Delaware." They may deduce the drift of events if he says no more than that he has a stomachache and thinks he's getting an ulcer.

The third reason you should restrain yourself during hostile takeovers is that there is another way for you to make profits from them—that is to buy stocks that would make good takeover candidates—provided, of course, they look like promising investments even if no one comes along to take them over.

One way to proceed is to buy stocks similar to those ones that are being gobbled up. When Philip Morris was about to make an offer for General Foods, stocks of other food companies suddenly jumped a few points. Apparently whatever interested raiders in the first company may well have been a feature of others in the same industry. This strategy only makes sense if you can buy the shares before stock prices of the companies get too far off the ground and if the stocks look like good investments apart from takeover possibilities. Fortunately, the same criteria used by Goldman Sachs to pinpoint stocks that are about to go up in price, also apply to stocks of interest to potential raiders. In fact, stocks meeting these criteria might even be good candidates for your IRA, since their potential for big losses is low. Perhaps the two most important shared traits are low price/earnings ratios and high book value per share.

Price/Earnings ratios. To determine the price/earnings (P/E) ratio, divide the share price of a stock by the company's annual net income per share for the most recent twelve months. For example, a company whose shares are currently quoted at $50 a share and whose net income per share is $5 would have a price/earnings ratio of 10. That's slightly less than the average P/E of all NYSE stocks at the end of 1985, which was 11. Thus this stock could be called a little lower than average. Actually it's not even necessary for you to calculate the P/E of a given stock since it is given daily with newspaper price quotations based on the most recent closing price for the shares.

Using the S & P 500, Goldman Sachs found that the 100 stocks with the lowest P/Es outperformed the index average by 22% in the six years through 1964. Takeover candidates are also more than likely to have below average P/E's before the raiders make their offers. Since the stock price is undervalued, raiders have more leeway to bid up the price without worrying that they are overpaying.

High book value per share in relation to stock price. This is even more important to rising market prices than the P/E ratio, the Goldman Sachs study found, and it is also very important to potential raiders as a reflection of the real value of their potential target company.

You must calculate this ratio yourself since it's not generally available for every stock. Here's how: You'll find a company's book value by dividing shareholders' equity in a company by the number of shares outstanding. The most recent figure for shareholders' equity is in the annual report. If the company doesn't identify the figure, you can calculate it from the balance sheet by subtracting total liabilities from total assets. In balance sheets these two figures are supposed to balance, and they do because companies add shareholder's equity to the bottom of the liabilities column. Shareholders' equity reflects the actual equity in the company owned by shareholders—the rest, more or less, is owed or mortgaged.

The bigger the shareholder's equity or book value per share, the more interesting the company to a raider. Look for stocks with a book value per share equal to or just slightly less than the current market price of the shares. Such stocks aren't apt to fall much in market price, which makes them fairly safe candidates for your IRA. Then if a raider comes along and the share price doubles, you'll collect the gains tax-free; if not, the fairly cheap stock might gradually rise in price anyway.

31

Stock Shorting

Something well known by professional traders that ordinary investors rarely figure out is that you can make money whether stock prices rise or fall—and the faster they move up or down the more money you can make. For this reason the professionals hate markets that stand still, even when prices are high.

Stock prices tend to move in long cycles. So, as surely as they go through a long upward climb, the day will no doubt come when they begin a long tumble. The pros will then begin to short stocks and the market. To short, you sell securities you don't own. If prices then drop, you make a profit.

It is possible for little investors to sell short too. Some custodians will even let you do it in a self-directed IRA, although the potential losses is equal to the premium so you should invest with caution. You can short almost anything—specific stocks, all the stocks on the New York Stock Exchange as a group, or even groups of stocks—like the oils or computer and technology stocks. Short trading is riskier than simply buying stocks, of course. You will lose all your money if prices go up instead of down. It makes sense, however, to keep a small short position. If prices fall, you will make money that can offset losses in the rest of your portfolio. If they rise, you will lose your money but that will simply reduce your overall profit. This is basic hedging, and when done in a limited way, is a conservative investment strategy.

In general, you can short specific stocks by buying puts through your existing brokerage house account, whether you use a discount or full-service broker. When you buy a put, you pay a premium for the right to put that stock to someone else at a specific price during a specific time period in the future. Here's how a put works: Let's say IBM is selling for $124 a share and you expect the price over the next few months to drop. Check the newspaper tables to find the price of a put. Perhaps you can buy the rights to "put" 100 shares of IBM to someone else next January at $125 a share for, say, $4.00 a share. (That would be the price quoted in the newspaper's Listed Options Quotations under Puts-Last, January.) Since puts trade in units of 100 shares, your premium would be $400. If the shares then dropped to, say, $110 by January, your profit, if you sold them, would be $15.00 a share or the strike price ($125) minus the selling price ($110) times 100 and minus your commissions. If the stock price was over your strike price when the option expired or when you attempted to sell the option, your puts would be worthless and you would lose your premium plus the buying commission.

Most brokers have a minimum commission for stock options. Charles Schwab & Co., for example, has a $31.50 minimum. Since you would have to pay that fee both to buy the options and then to sell them, assume a minimum of $63 for the trade.

You can also short the entire stock market—at least you can buy puts against several broad indexes—if you feel the market, in general, is going to fall. But you can't do this through all stock brokerage accounts. Technically these puts trade both as index options—which are listed on the same newspaper pages as options on specific stocks—and as options on commodity futures indexes—which are quoted on the commodities pages as Futures Options and are bought through commodities accounts.

Let's say you decide to short the Standard & Poor's

500 index and that it stands at 185, according to quotations in the newspaper. You decide to buy March (1986) puts with a strike price of 185, which carry a premium of 4.75 times $500 (the size of one put contract) adding up to $2375. Along the way to March, let's say the S & P 500 index dips to 170 and you decide to sell. The puts which you bought at 4.75 have now risen in value to say, 10.75. Your profit would be 6 (10.75 minus 4.75) times $500, or $3000, minus the commission. If, instead, the S & P rises above your strike price and stays there, you will lose all your money plus commission.

You can also buy or sell short the actual commodities futures for the S & P 500 and other indexes. But it is safer for individuals to stick with the options on the futures, since you can lose many times your margin requirement in the futures market.

You can buy futures options through Lind-Waldock or one of the other discount commodities brokers who advertise in the commodities pages. Most of these brokers are small Chicago companies offering little service except transacting the trades, which cost around $35 for the round trip—meaning purchase and eventual sale—of your single-option contract. Index options may also be purchased in the stock market—through most securities brokerage firms—and the mechanics of the transaction are basically the same.

There is another way to short the stock market that gives you an even bigger "bang for your buck." That is to short the shares of one of the big brokerage houses. Prices of these shares tend to turn up or down when the stock market turns, and their beta is higher than the market—meaning when the market drops, their price, proportionately, will probably drop harder. Conversely, the brokerage stocks also outpace the market in an upturn. Options on the stock of Merrill Lynch and of E. F. Hutton are publicly listed. You could buy these options through an ordinary stock brokerage account.

Buying puts isn't the only way to short stocks, but it is the simplest and safest, since you are only at risk for the amount of your investment. You can also sell, or write, calls, which are the opposite of puts. A call is the right to call a stock away from someone else at a specific price during a designated time period. If you write, or sell, or call, you are granting that right to someone else. If you are correct, and the price drops after you write the call, you collect the premium and lose nothing. If, instead, the stock price rises, you could be stuck honoring a call for the difference. Let's say you wrote a call for a stock at $10 a share and the price rose to $100 a share—the 100-share unit would cost you $90 times 100, or $9000. For that reason brokers have strict requirements on the amount you must keep on deposit against your call and concerning your own income level, net worth, and investing experience.

This isn't a game for amateurs, and stock shorting has little place in your IRA except possibly as a small hedge against inflation and rising interest rates when rates have been low and suddenly turn up (see Chapter 3).

32
Hedging with Options

Can you protect your whole stock portfolio against a possible downturn in the market and still hold onto the stocks? The answer is yes—for a price, you can do it with put options on stockmarket indexes or subindexes of stocks in specific industries.

Individual stocks in some major industrial categories like technology, transportation, and oil can be hedged with puts on subindexes of those industries quoted under "Index Options" in your newspaper. These aren't a perfect hedge, but many professionals use the Computer Technology Index on the American Stock Exchange to hedge their IBM holdings. About half of that index is represented by IBM.

When you are thoroughly convinced the stock market has begun a long-term downslide, it might make more sense to sell your stocks—particularly if you hold them inside your IRA—and put most of your money into the money market, coupled, possibly, with a small investment in put options. But what if you own the stock outside of your IRA and you are just a month or so away from being able to report your big stockmarket gains as long-term capital gains (taxable at a maximum rate of 20% of your profits). Your dilemma is that if you sell your stocks immediately to avoid a price drop, you must report short-term capital gains (taxable at a maximum rate of 50%—or 35%–38% under tax reform). In such a case it may make sense to hold your stocks for the long-term period and hedge your investments by buying puts on each of the stocks in your portfolio that have publicly listed-and-traded put options. These options would give you the right to put a specific stock to someone else at a specific price during a specified period in the future. If you buy a put and the price of the underlying stock drops—which is what you expect—you will make a profit equal to the difference between the prices.

But under the tax law, buying the puts would mean starting the counting period toward long-term capital gains again. You would then have to hold onto both the put and the underlying stock for another six months plus a day. An alternative, and a good one if you have a diversified stock portfolio, is to sell the entire stock market short by buying put options on one of the market indexes. Another way to do this would be to buy a put option on the Standard & Poor's 500 index or another general market index listed in the futures option market. Options on indexes are sold both ways. Futures options are options on the indexes as traded in the commodities futures markets rather than options on the indexes themselves.

In general, index options are a bit cheaper than options on the indexes as traded in the commodities futures market. Prices for futures options are quoted on the commodities pages of your newspaper while prices for index options and options on subindexes like technology stocks are quoted on the same page as stock options.

Let's say that the Standard & Poor's 100-stock index currently stands at 181. And let's say that quotations for that index option, which is publicly traded on the Chicago Board, include a six-month-from-now (January) put option with a strike price of 180 quoted at 3¾. That translates into $3.75 a unit (puts on 100 shares) or $375 for the 100-share put contract. If you buy the index options put for $375 and the stockmarket rises—or at least the prices of the 100 largest stocks as measured by the S & P 100 index rise or stay at the same level—

you're out $375. But you can claim the lost premium for tax purposes against the capital gains you make on the stock.

All options on broad markets like the S & P 100 or New York Stock Exchange index are treated for capital gains purposes as if 60% of the gains or losses are long-term capital gains and 40% are short term. That's true whether you hold the options for mere seconds or longer than six months and a day, the holding period required to qualify for long-term capital gains treatment of stock-market profits. Profits on the special industry subindexes, on the other hand, are treated like capital gains on options for specific stocks. If the gains are realized before the six-months-and-one-day cutoff, they are short term; if they meet the time requirement, they're long term.

Getting back to the case under discussion, if the S & P 100 index tumbled back to 170 instead of rising by the January expiration date, you would be able to sell your option for the 170-a-unit strike price, pocketing $1,000 (100 times the $10 difference between the 180 strike price and the 170 termination price) minus your initial $375 and minus brokerage commissions of around $65. The $560 you cleared in this transaction could offset all or part of the losses in your stock portfolio realized when you held onto the stock during the market downturn.

PART VI

Some Investment Alternatives

SOMETIMES, when interest rates are rising and market prices are dropping, an investor just isn't satisfied with the return offered by stock or bonds and is willing to take on substantial added risk for bigger gains.

For the most part, investments of this sort are not appropriate and possibly not even legal for your IRA. Collectibles and antiques, for example, are not permitted for IRAs. But outside your IRA there are investments you can sample that historically have shown big gains when other markets begin to founder.

At such times inflation is usually beginning to heat up, a circumstance in which you may find it advantageous to call into play a sort of investment that can even be called speculation—since you are rarely certain you won't lose most or all of your money. Conversely, profits are also possible in multiples of your original investment, along with tax writeoffs that could double your profits if you are lucky. To be sure, there are often ways to hedge against big losses, but such hedging can pare profit potential down to minimal levels.

Some of these speculative inflation-linked investments include *commodities futures*—from wheat to gold; *options on those futures* (which are a little less risky); *investment partnerships* in real estate, oil and even farms of various types, which may or may not also be tax shelters; *real property* like your own home, *antiques*, *art* and *collectibles*.

Tax reform will clearly reduce the tax benefits of limited partnerships, particularly in real estate, but the risk, potentiality for big profits, and even tax shelter advantages will still apply to a greater or lesser extent.

For the most part such investments aren't allowed in your IRA, and because of the potential for big losses—plus the fact that you hardly need a tax shelter within your tax shelter—you probably wouldn't want to put them in your IRA even if you were allowed. You can, however, put shares of commodities funds and pools in your IRA, and these are slightly less volatile than the actual futures (See Chapter 9). In addition, some big brokerage houses are offering limited partnerships without tax shelter benefits that invest in non-leveraged income-producing real estate. Thus you can put real estate in your IRA as well as commodities.

Some of these limited partnerships and funds promise profits far in excess of what is possible in even the highest-yielding bonds, but there is also added risk.

The same is true of collectibles, art, and antiques. Auction prices for such items skyrocketed with inflation in the late 1970s, but a few years later many of them couldn't be sold at any price. One compensation, though,

SOME INVESTMENT ALTERNATIVES

is that you can still enjoy the art or collectible—assuming you bought it because you like it—even if there's no current market for it.

Similarly, many American homeowners made astronomical profits when they sold their houses in the late 1970's, but when inflation dropped so did housing prices. By year-end 1985, many people who bought homes as an investment in the late 1970's suddenly found they could only sell them at a loss. However, homes could again become a good investment if interest rates start to rise and inflation flames up again. But you can't put your own home in your IRA anyway.

33
Commodities Futures and Options

Commodities may be regarded as the Las Vegas of the investment world. You can lose more money in commodities futures—in a few days or even a few minutes—than anywhere else in the public investment world. And if the futures market is Las Vegas, it's first cousin—the market for options on commodities futures—is Atlantic City. You can't lose more money than you put up in these options, and they come in smaller pieces than most futures contracts, but you can still triple your profits or wipe out in a matter of days.

For the most part there is no place in most IRAs for commodities—although some brokerage houses will let you put shares of commodities mutual funds in your IRA account (see Chapter 9). What's more, there's nothing about commodities that would let you profit from playing the averages—as you could in the stock market by buying funds such as the Standard & Poor's 500-stock index, which consistently outperforms most money managers. Most options, for example, close "out of the money," meaning no profit for the option holder. Any attempt at random selection is doomed to failure, and commodities indexes don't mean much, since most lump together agricultural commodities and financial futures—the two entities that move in unrelated directions.

You can pay a professional commodities trader to man-

SOME INVESTMENT ALTERNATIVES

age your futures account, and you stand a good chance of coming out ahead. But even the pros sometimes go broke. And most traders with good track records aren't interested in your account if it's smaller than $100,000. Beyond that you pay dearly for managed accounts. A strong word of caution is appropriate here. Such managed accounts became the pets of commodities boiler rooms of telephone salesmen in the late 1970's. Prospective clients were led to believe that they were dealing with seasoned traders and often were given the impression—with the help of tape-recorded sounds—that they were being called from a commodities exchange floor. In fact, the salesmen were fronting for elaborate scams and high-pressure sales organizations that used inexperienced traders or no research at all and often did not even bother to invest their clients' deposits in commodities at all. The Commodities Futures Trading Commission closed out the worst offenders, but boiler room-type telephone sales and hired-off-the-street salesmen still exist. So if you do decide on a manage commodities account, be certain to get a personal reference for the trader from someone you actually know, and ask him to supply you with his trading records, which must be kept for the CFTC.

Besides futures markets and options markets there are commodities mutual funds or pools, which avoid some of the worst pitfalls of this type of investment; but even here management fees are high.

Considering all this, the watchword is caution. If you decide to dabble at all in commodities, you should bone up on a specific commodity or two, subscribing to commodities news services, collecting crop reports and other materials from the U.S. Department of Agriculture, and improving your understanding of such subjects as international trade and what is happening to the U.S. dollar.

If you select coffee, for example, you'll soon find yourself worrying about weather conditions and crop prospects in Brazil along with a variety of other concerns. If the crop doesn't freeze, coffee prices tumble, particularly if there has been speculation favoring a possible freeze. If the freeze does come as expected, coffee prices rise since a shortage of Brazilian coffee is likely. You'll also learn about blends and how much African coffee goes into drip blends compared to percolator blends and if more people are buying Mr. Coffee-type machines than use the drip method.

Having armed yourself with knowledge, you may then decide to speculate on coffee in the futures market, going long or buying contracts in the future if you expect prices to go up; going short or selling contracts in the future if you expect prices to go down. To do this you must open a margin account for futures trading—there are no accounts in this business that aren't margin accounts, which are different in concept from margin in the securities business (see Chapter 13). Just to open the account you will probably have to put up some money on deposit with your broker—say $20,000. From that you make a down payment on the futures contract you select; the margin rate—usually 5% to 20%—is set by the exchange on which the commodity is traded. Typical margin deposits are around $1000. At that point you technically have bought, or sold, a huge contract in the commodity—say 25,000 pounds of copper. Now you watch the price quoted for that commodity in the month your contract expires. Let's say you bought a December copper contract on the N.Y. Commodity Exchange (Comex), and the price you paid was 64 cents a pound. If the price of copper dropped one cent the following day on your single contract, you would be out $250 in a single day.

In fact, one penny movements in commodities can mean big profits or big losses for you. For sugar a penny costs $1,120, in pork bellies it's $380, and in silver $500. Commodity prices can jump as much as a penny in one day, although the exchanges have limits on the amount

SOME INVESTMENT ALTERNATIVES

a price may move in a day that are generally smaller than a penny.

You can reduce your exposure to some degree by playing spreads between exchanges. Here you buy a commodity on one exchange and simultaneously sell it on another. This is the only way commodities futures should ever be played in an IRA, and it will be difficult to find an IRA custodian who will permit even this. But this type of speculation involves even more research than playing straight futures. Let's say you find that the only wheat the U.S. is exporting is being sold to the Soviet Union; from your research you know that the Russians prefer hard-red-winter wheat and that more such wheat sells on the exchange of the Kansas City Board of Trade than on the Chicago Board of Trade exchange. From this you deduce that the price of wheat in Kansas City will rise faster than in Chicago and you create a spread, by buying a Kansas City wheat contract and selling a Chicago one for the same month. Now if the price of wheat should drop, you are protected in Chicago; if it should rise, you will profit in Kansas City. And if it should rise faster in Kansas City—where you've bought—than in Chicago, you'll make $50 for each penny of difference—as if you had just bought the Chicago contract.

The advantage, of course, is that you are protected against huge losses by your spread (although you also will lose $50 for each penny difference if the spread narrows instead of widening). Another advantage is that margin deposits are less when you take a spread, permitting you to expose less money or to acquire more contracts.

Another way to limit potential losses is to buy options on the commodities futures rather than futures contracts. You buy these options as puts and calls, just like stock options, and unlike futures contracts, you can't lose more money than you actually put up.

34

Collectibles: the Market Inflation Made

Something amazing happened in the 1970s that few investment professionals recognized. Inflation produced a whole new investment market: collectibles. And today the most popular collectible—limited-edition collector's plates—trades on its own plate exchange with price quotations investors can get over an 800-number.

One can only assume the conditions that produced the inflation-fueled race into gold, stamps, coins, antiques, and art in the 1970s created a demand larger than existing tangibles of value could fill. It spilled over into porcelain plates that a few European manufacturers were making, in limited edition, as a gift item. Plates apparently had the right characteristics to satisfy the demand: they weren't terribly expensive (mostly $7 to $75 when bought as new issues), they appealed to middle-aged, middle-class women who had money to spend, you could display them proudly, they appeared to be in limited supply and they were easy to understand.

In the early 1970s the stock market foundered on a wave of inflation that shook out many of the Wall Street brokerage firms. Casualties were high among small investors. Meanwhile the race into collector plates had begun to heat up. The market for this item developed in the late 1960s. It wasn't until 1969 that any of the few existing collectors' plates showed any sudden increase in resale value. In that year Bing & Grendahl started a second series of annual collector's plates, and Wedgewood entered the market with a plate series. By Christmas the Bing & Grendahl plate, issued at $9.75, was selling for $65 through some simple back-issue price sheets used by gift dealers. The Wedgewood plate, issued at $10, was quoted at $38 by Christmas. Later, commenting on the phenomenon of the 1970s plate market December 1981, the *Wall Street Journal* ran a front-page article with a headline reading: "While you were going under, Granny got in at $100, got out at $450."

The Bradford Exchange began issuing price quotes on the plates and set up its Bradex Index in 1974. Not surprisingly, the exchange was a brainchild of the late Chicago financier and insurance tycoon, John MacArthur. As inflation and high interest rates cooled after 1981, prices on the Bradex dropped steadily through the end of 1985. But according to the Bradex, demand for plates, both new and not so new, continued at a steady pace.

As a gauge to how inflation works in the marketplace to create value, there is no better example than plates. And when inflation and interest rates rise again, a quick reading of this chapter will be a refresher course in inflation-related investment behavior which will no doubt create more new markets in response to changing conditions.

It's hard to take collector's plates seriously with all those kittens, bunnies, and pink-cheeked children. One imagines John MacArthur, the financier's son and chairman of the Bradex as well as publisher of *Harper's Magazine*, taking a stiff gulp when he writes items like the following in his monthly plate market analysis: "Diddle, Diddle Dumpling posted an 83.7 percent increase over the last reporting period." Diddle, Diddle Dumpling is a plate showing a little boy with his teddy bear issued in 1984 by Reco International, a U.S. based plate manufacturer.

But make no mistake, today there is a real market for buying and reselling these plates—sometimes at a big profit and sometimes at a big loss. Of course, the Bradex isn't exactly the Amex, or American Stock Exchange. For one thing it is privately owned and not only acts as a trading floor for old collector plates but also acts as a plate dealer, hawking new plates by direct mail and late night television advertising. Since it introduced its computerized trading floor in late 1981, it has created a liquid market for collector's plates. Plate collectors open accounts, call for plate price quotes, and can instantly buy or sell by phone with plate floor traders.

The rules that emerged in the plate market are unlike those that control the stock market and equally unlike those that rule the antiques market. Just in case you hope to make a killing in plates here are a few tips: Sell plates when they are two to five years old. Unlike art and antiques that tend to appreciate as years go by, collector's plates tend to peak in price from two to four years after they are issued. After that, prices plateau or drop, and with less demand, even scarce plates are harder to sell. In this market oddities and misprints have no value. When the postoffice prints the art on a stamp upside down, the misprinted stamps frequently soar in value in the stamp market. Not so with misprinted plates. Sometimes the backstamp, with the plate's name, year, and limited edition number contains an error. Instead of adding to value this could render the plate unsellable.

In new issues look for artists who are household words— in middle-class households. Some of the most popular plates have come from art by Norman Rockwell, Berta Hummel, and John McClelland. But several plates by Salvador Dali, in contrast, were a failure. According to Emil S. Polk, former president of the Collector Platemaker's Guild, "The vast majority of women who collect plates want an artist that they know, and they don't know Dali. They know Norman Rockwell. Period."

SOME INVESTMENT ALTERNATIVES

Size of the limited edition matters only if it is very large or very small. In general, edition size hasn't proved to have much to do with future market price. Very small editions—like the often-handmade, 1000-copy issues of Venito Flair—tend to be too small to attract attention. Furthermore, since this particular company sells handpainted collector's plates—most others are done by a decal process much like lithograph—the quality can vary from plate to plate, causing confusion.

PART VII

Technology and Your Investments

Technology has changed the rules of investing for professionals and amateurs alike. The computers that help professional securities traders make split-second decisions are available for home use in almost the same form. They have made possible virtually instant calculation to derive latest prices, high, lows and closing prices for stocks, bonds, and commodities traded not only on the big exchanges but also in smaller over-the-counter markets.

For the investor this translates into next-day availability of price quotes and closing information through daily newspapers and even cable television. It permits huge amounts of information to be tabulated weekly in publications like *Barron's*, which is available on many newsstands each Saturday morning with the weekly averages from the Friday afternoon close.

There is no question that home computers make possible feats that previously were inconceivable for little investors. In fact, for a price you can get nearly all the same information as professional research analysts, and you can buy or sell stocks by pressing a few buttons much like professional traders. Make no mistake, this can make a big difference. The speed of being able to call up a stock, bond or commodity price quotation in seconds and then quickly buy or sell the stock or other security puts the tools of the professionals at your fingertips.

But speed and quick quotations aren't the only advantage of using your home computer for investment. Your computer makes possible nearly professional record keeping, and you can keep tabs on all your investments with spreadsheets and other sophisticated devices.

And through your computer you can now tap into big data banks that permit you to do relatively sophisticated stockmarket analysis at home. The advantage of this is that even small investors can perform do-it-yourself research and, should they so desire, bypass the higher-cost full-service stockbrokers. Most computer trading programs link into discount brokers with commissions that are lower than regular securities brokers. The difference is that discount brokers don't offer the research and advice that you get from a regular broker.

Should you consider doing-it-yourself by computer? The following considerations might influence your decision:

Do you already have a home computer? Purchase of the basic computer can run well over $2000, depending on the model you select. In order to invest by computer you will also need a modem (a device that attaches your computer to the telephone so that you can tap into data banks and quotation services) and software (for example, you would need it to do spreadsheets and other record keeping on the computer). Since some software works with some computers and not others, you should research your needs before buying the basic system. In addition you will need to buy the information and trading services: the charges for them characteristically include a one-time buy-in fee and use charges for each minute that you are on line.

How much background have you in basic investment and money management? While very sophisticated information is currently available, some basic knowledge is needed for you to understand it. For example, it is possible to get summaries of official documents like prospectuses and annual 10-K filings by computer. But this does you little good if you have no idea what a prospectus is, let alone how to read and analyze it.

Fortunately, however, much basic research and analysis involves simple logic and common sense. Indeed, with this book alone it should be possible—if you read and study the chapters on research and information gathering—to make some basic investment decisions. But you must at least invest the time.

How much money do you have to invest? If you expect to invest this year, say, $500 in your first IRA, a $3000 investment in computer equipment, software, and services doesn't make much sense, even though your computer can be written off for tax purposes. On the other hand, if you expect that over the next, say, ten years you will have substantial funds to invest, both the money and time you spend on a computer may be well worthwhile.

If you intend to do your own research and buy and sell securities through a discount broker, a computer system is almost essential. At the very least you should have a subscription to the *Wall Street Journal* or *Investor's Daily*, along with *Barron's*, a weekly tabloid that has almost every statistic and average imaginable for the week ended on the past Friday.

However, unless you want to spend all of your time cutting out articles and keeping extensive files, you can't duplicate the services available over your computer. If you have the Dow Jones Information Service, for example, and you want information on General Motors, here's a sample of the data available on your computer: First, you can call up a directory of every story about General Motors that has run on the Dow Jones News Ticker or in the *Wall Street Journal* or *Barron's* for the past ten years, starting with the most recent—often something that ran on the electronic ticker just minutes before you called it up on your computer. Next, you can call up a copy of an entire story, assuming it is either fairly recent or fairly important. These stories will give you a good sense of what's been going on at the company.

Assuming you want to explore the company further, you can now call up statistics on the company that range from the obvious— earnings history, revenues, dividends—to the obscure. If you so desire, you can call up the stock's so-called beta for declining markets, which will tell you how that stock historically has performed in bad markets—whether its price drops faster or slower than the rest of the market, for example. You can then call up summaries of some of the company's recent filings with the Securities & Exchange Commission, such as the previously mentioned prospectus or 10-K filing. Here you will find everything from the amount of stock held by insiders; to recent court suits against the company; to alleged risks that could cause problems for the company, its stock, or its stockholders.

DO-IT-YOURSELF ANALYSIS

Let's say you decide you do want to try a little analysis on your own. Where do you start? Probably by subscribing to one of the software services that permit you—on line—to sort through long lists of stocks for qualities that are important to you. Let's say you are looking for stocks that have a price-earnings ratio below 7 (meaning they are cheap, according to this analytical ratio), that have reported no annual losses in the past two years, and that have grown at a rate of at least 10% in the past five years. By using the software described in the next chapter it is now possible for a small investor, at home and on his own computer, to do much of the analysis that once could only be acquired through a full service broker with a big research department.

Home computer systems also can be useful for investors who use full-service brokers as well as those who use discount brokers. You are headed into trouble if you don't have the capacity to monitor the professionals you hire to make your investment decisions or advise you. While there is less need to keep an eye on the market minute-to-minute if you've delegated the responsibility to someone else, you need to be able to ask the right questions. For example, if your stockbroker advised investment in a wide range of oil and energy stocks and you took his advice, you should keep an eye on the price of oil and the performance of your stocks. If the price of oil has been sliding for several weeks and he has not advised you to sell, you should be in a position to ask him why. He may have a good reason or he may not. And if a change in investment advisor ever is called for, you should have the information needed to make the right decision.

WAR GAMES

If you decide to take the plunge and buy a computer, one way to start is with some computer investing games. Games are available for your computer that create hypothetical investments and market conditions. You learn investment strategies, how various types of investments work, and how to use your computer all at one time, and it only costs you the price of the game.

The fastest and most entertaining games involve trade in commodities futures, which is also the fastest and most volatile investment around. Good ones include "COMEX: The Game," which is available from the Comex Options Department in New York for $69.95; "Tycoon," from Blue Chip Software, and "Speculator," from O.C.O. Software. "Millionare" is a stockmarket game from Blue Chip Software. The same company makes "Squire," in which you can select everything from stocks to interest rate futures, and "Baron," a real estate investment game.

35
Managing Investments by Home Computer

The basis of most investment software packages is the electronic spreadsheet. The idea is that the investor places onto the spreadsheet numbers and formulas which then can be called up by themselves or in combination with other groups of numbers and formulas. Multiple calculations occur instantly, linking or combining the various formulas and figures. Using such electronic spreadsheets, an investor can test strategies, track gains or losses in his securities portfolio, compare brokerage costs and other fees, and keep on top of target prices at which he intends to buy or sell each security.

By combining a software spreadsheet and an information service that supplies, say, price quotations, the investor can call up both his list of target prices and current on-line prices at the same time. The software program will then flag each stock that requires action. Software packages with spreadsheets are now available from a number of banks and brokerage houses in combination with bank-by-computer services. Some are only available for use on specific computers. Some involve an entry fee and others don't.

The first spreadsheet accounting program was introduced by VisiCalc in 1978. That program and a later one, the SuperCalc, can be purchased at stores offering computer software. More sophisticated (and expensive) software programs like "Symphony" from Lotus Development Corp., and "Framework" by Ashton-Tate, make possible even more professional analysis. With these, for example, you can isolate a group of stocks from your spreadsheet based on a shared characteristic such as price/earnings ratio, and you can rearrange the list by size of earnings.

These software programs can be used in connection with on-line information services that connect to your computer through a telephone and modem or a broadcasting device. The programs come in the form of a disc, so it's important to have a computer that is compatible with the program you select. Many can only be used with IBM computers or those that are totally compatible, like Compac.

By taking advantage of the various data banks and information services, the little investor can now do the type of research on his own that simply isn't possible with a paper and pencil.

36

Getting Price Quotes and Research

GETTING PRICE QUOTES

Once you've invested in a stock or commodity, it suddenly becomes important to know where the price of that stock is quoted—right this minute. With today's technology that's possible even for a little investor on a limited budget who doesn't have a computer.

Time was that only brokers and other big investors could afford what are called real time quotes. Only a few years ago it cost $500 and more a month for a service that would transmit stock, bond, or commodities prices to you instantly from the exchanges. Beyond that there were large, separate monthly fees charged by the exchanges. The New York Stock Exchange, for example, charged $90 a month to make its price quotations available. Then in 1984 the exchanges dropped their prices, and now the NYSE monthly fee, for example, is $7.50. In any case, advances in technology have made it possible for you to receive price quotations at substantially lower rates over your home computer, your television set, your telephone and even over new portable receivers made specifically for price quotations.

The most portable means of keeping in touch with your investments are new devices that receive market quotations from signals broadcast over FM radio waves and by satellite. One such price quotation service is supplied by a subsidiary of the Lotus Development Corporation. Quotations are received on a little battery-operated, hand-held device called Quotrec which costs about $400. The broadcast service costs $30 a month and up, depending on how many exchanges you want to monitor. You can choose stocks from all the big exchanges and NASDAQ, as well as most commodities or options quotations. One drawback is that your Quotrec won't work if you get too far away from New York City or one of the twelve other cities where Lotus's quotation service operates. The quotations are broadcast by FM signals which can't be received more than thirty or so miles from the broadcast point.

How instant are Lotus's quotations? Quotes delivered by FM signals can lag the actual tape by about three minutes. That's not as instant as some of the high-priced services that go by telephone into your computer. But it's much faster than the 15-minute delay characteristic of quotations delivered by the lower-priced services like the Dow Jones Information Service. The 15-minute delay still applies to quotes from Telemet, which are received over the Pocket Quote Pro, a hand-held device that is similar to Quotrec. Pocket Quote Pro costs $395 and the annual fee for the quotation service is $300.

Computer-delivered services include the Dow Jones service, which can be attached to your computer by telephone modem and delivers immediate quotes for stocks, bonds, and other issues listed on the major stock exchanges. However, it doesn't offer NASDAQ or other over-the-counter stock prices, commodities prices, or other options prices. To attach the Dow Jones service to your home computer costs a $75 entrance charge, a monthly $18.50 subscription price, a $3-a-month service charge, and fees for each minute you're on-line that range up to

90 cents a minute during prime time when the exchanges are open.

The Telemet quotations available with the Pocket Quote Pro can also be received by computer. The service for this is the Radio Exchange, which costs $279 to subscribe plus the same $300-a-year fee charged with the Pocket Quote Pro. The Telemet service offers a wide range of quotations, including over-the-counter stocks, commodities futures, and options.

Lotus's quotations can also be received on your home computer—if it is IBM-compatible—by acquiring a device and subscribing to a service known as Signal. Signal costs $595 for the FM receiver and attachment for your IBM computer. It must be used with either the Lotus 1-2-3 or the Symphony software programs. You then pay to Lotus $80 a month plus an additional $20 for each exchange you want to monitor.

Some brokers also offer security price quotations for you to receive by computer. Charles Schwab & Co., for example, includes the Dow Jones Information Service price quotations in a software and trading package it sells investors. And Fidelity Group of Boston has a system called Fidelity Investor Express which connects to your personal computer by telephone modem. Fidelity charges $50 plus $15 a month and overtime.

There are yet other ways to get stock quotations during the trading day: Financial News Network, for example, broadcasts prices all day long over cable television. The problem is that you must sit and wait for your stock to roll by, and there is a 15-minute delay. Schwab has a quotation service that uses your touch-tone telephone. At one time anyone could subscribe by paying an annual fee of $20, which entitled them, for a five-cent charge, to get the last-sale price and net change over the phone by punching up the right numbers plus a symbol for their security. Today the service is only available to Schwab customers. Fidelity Investments of Boston also has a touch-tone telephone service that monitors prices on 8000 stocks but, like Schwab, it is only available to Fidelity's customers.

Without subscribing to any special service you can get price quotes by touch-tone telephone from Dow Jones. You simply call 1-800-257-0437 to sign up and get the needed information, then you are charged 50 cents a minute for your time on-line if you are calling locally; if you use the 800 number you pay $1 a minute.

GETTING INVESTMENT INFORMATION

Where can you get information to use in your research? Where can you go for basic information like research reports on various securities from Wall Street analysts, financial news, and fundamental statistics on the companies or securities that interest you?

Such information is conveniently available if you subscribe to a data bank. These on-line services have certain exclusive data along with investment services like Media General that are available through several data banks. Media General supplies up-to-date basic information such as price-earnings ratios, earnings histories, and asset on values on publicly-traded companies. The Media General Service is offered both by The Source and by Dow Jones Information Systems.

Beyond that, some of the databases are included in on-line and software services provided by brokers—like the package offered by Charles Schwab & Co., which uses databases from both Warner Computer Systems and Dow Jones Information Systems.

Here are some of the big data banks and what they offer:

Dow Jones Information Systems. Also known as Dow Jones News/Retrieval, has thirty-five databases. Among its offerings are financial information excerpted from publicly filed documents on 9400 companies from Disclosure II; consensus earnings forecasts for 3000 companies; current and historic news from the *Wall Street Journal* (which Dow Jones publishes); news from the Dow Jones news wires, which receive most releases from public companies. Costs include a $75 one-time password fee and per-minute charges for on-line time. It will cost you $1.20 a minute, for example, to get on-line business news during prime time, when the exchanges are open. Evenings you can get price quotes for 15 cents a minute. Contact Dow Jones in Princeton, New Jersey.

The Source Investor Services. Owned by the people who publish *Readers' Digest*, has almost as many services as Dow Jones and also has facilities for 24-hour stock trading by computer through Spear Securities. It costs $49.95 for a password and then you pay by the on-line hour, with a $10-a-month minimum. The Source is in McLean, Virginia.

CompuServe. Offers Executive Information Service, which has a number of investment data bases, and a few investment services are provided with its basic Consumer Information Service as well. The Consumer Service costs an initial $39.95 plus hourly charges for on-line usage. There is a $10-a-month minimum if you want to use the Executive Information Service. CompuServe is in Columbus, Ohio.

Warner Computer Systems. Offers a variety of investment services in the Warner Data Bases. Warner has a $48 password fee plus per-minute charges. It charges no monthly minimum, but there is a $1 minimum charge for each time you log on and connect with the system. Warner Computer Systems is in Hackensack, New Jersey.

37
Trading Securities by Computer

It is now possible to trade stocks much like the professionals do, but on your own home computer. You can buy or sell with the press of a few buttons, using one of the computer trading and research services offered by dozens of major banks and discount brokers.

Most of these services permit you to research and place trading orders any time you please, and in general, if you place an order while the stock exchanges are open, your shares can be acquired in a matter of minutes. If your order is received in off-hours, most services will place your order on an exchange when it opens, at the opening or going price.

However, twenty-four-hour trading privileges are offered by at least one service. That is The Source, a computer data service run by *Reader's Digest*, which uses Spear Securities, a Los Angeles-based firm, to provide on-line, all-hours trading along with various information services. The service costs $49.95 plus $20 a month. The phone number for The Source is 800-336-3366, and for Spear Securities it is 800-821-1902.

What do you need to subscribe to such services? To attach your computer to the data bank computer over a telephone line, you will need a modem, which may cost you $200 and more. You may also need a separate "dedicated" telephone line for the modem. It is also important to have the right computer—one that is compatible with software packages which can be used to keep track of your securities portfolio and monitor your account. Charles Schwab's package, for example, can be used with the IBM PC or XT, or the Apple 2-E or 2-C, or another computer totally compatible with these.

What advantages are there to doing your own trading and research by home computer? Since these services all involve discount brokers, with trading commissions below that of regular brokers, there can be overall cost savings, even after taking into account the costs of on-line equipment and computer services. Also, where actual stock price quotations are immediately available to the computer trader, his ability to make instant sales and purchases can spell a lot of difference in today's volatile stock and options markets. According to Spear Securities most orders they receive can be executed in two seconds.

Glossary/Index

Annual Report (Yearly financial statements of a company, usually also containing names of officers and directors, and a review of the past year's business. *Also see Ten-K*.), 166, 176

Annuities (Annual payment of an allowance or income on an investment, often resulting from a single large payment from an insurance policy, pension plan or retirement account.), 1, 19, 36, 76

    Fixed Rate (Annuity on which the amount of the annual payment is fixed, thus based on a fixed rate of return on the initial investment.), 19

    Individual Retirement, IRA (One official form of Individual Retirement Arrangement as specified by the IRS is an Individual Retirement Annuity, the name given any form of IRA set up through an insurance company. Such "annuities" need not make annual payments and can work much like a savings account during working years with various alternatives at retirement, including a lump sum payment or regular annual payments.), 1, 19, 36, 76

    Lifetime (Lifetime annuities make guaranteed payments to the annuity holder during his lifetime, regardless of how long the holder lives.), 19

    Variable (Variable annuities make payments to the annuity holder that can rise or fall with differences on the rate of return on the underlying investment.), 76

Arbitrage, Arbitrager (Today commonly refers to risk arbitrage, which involves speculation on the outcome of mergers or other events on the value of certain securities that are purchased or sold by the arbitrager in great volume. Classic arbitrage, on the other hand, involves large volume securities transactions where there is a small profit with no risk, such as buying securities on one exchange and simultaneously selling them on another where the price is fractionally higher.), 162, 185–189

Barron's (Weekly financial tabloid newspaper with numerous financial statistics for the preceding week that is published by Dow Jones & Co.), 163

Bond Ratings, 126, 127

Bonds (Securities that companies or government bodies issue to borrow money, usually at a fixed rate, that they pay back with interest to bond holders on a regular basis over a number of years or when the bond matures. Corporate bonds usually come in $1000 denominations.), 119–144

    Accumulation (Bonds that accumulate interest unpaid until the bond matures, thus producing compounded interest.), 140–145

    Convertible (Bonds that can be converted into stock.) 35, 36, 135

    Corporate (Bonds issued by companies.), 134–136

    Ginnie Maes, GNMAs (Government-backed mortgage securities issued through the Government National Mortgage Association.), 130–133

    Government and Government Agency (Bonds issued by the U.S. Treasury, such as Treasury Bills, Bonds and Notes, to raise funds for government agencies such as the GNMA. These securities are backed by the U.S. government, but this can get tricky. The Federal National Mortgage Assocation, which issues FNMA mortgage-backed securities similar to GNMAs, is not, for example, a government agency, it's a Congressionally-chartered public company. Thus, FNMAs, or Fannie Maes as they are called, are not Federal government insured in the way that Ginnie Maes are.), 34, 35, 122, 123, 130–133

    Junk (Bonds with very low ratings for security that must, as a result, pay very high rates of interest.), 3, 124, 125, 135, 146

    Municipals (Securities issued by cities, directly or indirectly, that receive special tax treatment permitting their holders, under some circumstances, to pay no federal tax on the interest income.), 137–139

        Returns compared with taxable bonds, 138

    Mutual funds (Bond mutual funds acquire large portfolios of bonds that are purchased by mutual fund holders in the form of equal shares, each representing a portion of the whole portfolio. As bonds mature new ones are purchased.), 99, 124, 125, 148, 149

    Unit trusts (Bond unit trusts acquire large bond portfolios all bought at the same time. When they mature the proceeds are distributed to shareholders.), 146–149

    U.S. Savings (Savings bonds are issued by the U.S. Treasury in small denominations ($50–$10,000) to permit purchase by individuals.), 142–145

    Zero-Coupon (Bonds that accumulate dividends that aren't paid out until the bond matures.), 140–142

Brokers (Technically, brokers represent the buyer in a transaction in contrast to agents, such as insurance agents, who represent the seller.)

    Commodities (Commodities brokers can operate from a full-service securities brokerage firm or in specialized commodities operations.), 110

    Discount (Discount brokers operate in most securities fields and will execute trades at rates lower than full-service brokers. In general,

discount brokers don't offer research or investment advice.), 111–112
Full-Service (Full-service brokers offer research and investment advice and charge rates higher than discount brokers.), 108–110, 111–112
Insurance (Insurance brokers represent insurance buyers and generally can sell the products of a number of different insurance companies.), 76
Securities (Securities brokers sell stocks, bonds and often other securities including commodities futures and unit trust shares.), 108–112
Stock (Stock brokers sell stocks, though the term is often used for securities brokers who may sell other securities as well.), 108–112

Capital (This is the net worth of a company, or the amount of money invested in the company. In general practice, capital usually refers to investment in stock or equity, or the total amount you have to invest.), 42–44, 173
Calls (See Options)
Capital Gains (See Income)
Cash Value Per Share (The net worth of shareholders' equity in a company divided by the number of outstanding shares. See Net Worth.), 162
Certificate of Deposit, CD (Security sold to an investor by a bank or thrift institution that pays a fixed rate over a specified period of time, usually 10 years or less.), 4, 24, 30, 31, 43, 52–54, 119–123
CFTC, Commodities Futures Trading Commission (A federal agency that regulates the commodities exchanges and administers federal commodities law.), 201
Chicago Board of Trade (One of the commodities exchanges, based in Chicago.), 203
COMEX, New York Commodities Exchange (One of the commodities exchanges, based in New York City.), 202
Commercial Paper (Money market securities that are corporate IOUs sold to institutions and other investors to raise short-term cash.), 128
Commodities (Commodities are agricultural, industrial, and financial goods that are sold over exchanges as "futures" for future delivery. Investors can buy and sell "futures" without taking delivery of the "actuals" or physical commodity, which can be acquired through the exchange by a manufacturer or other who wants the physical commodity by holding a "buy" contract on the futures contract to maturity.), 200–203
    Futures (See Futures)
    Mutual Funds (Commodities contracts are assembled into large portfolios and sold to investors in the form of mutual fund shares.), 81, 82
    Options (See Options)
    Pools (Commodities pools are similar to commodities mutual funds, but start with a fixed investment and are then closed to new investors.), 200–203
Compound Interest
    Tables by Year and Rate, 7, 8
    Years to Offset 10% Penalty, 15
    Effect of frequency of compounding, 30

INDEX

Custodian, IRA (*See Trustee, IRA*)

Data bank, computer (Large assembly of information stored for computer users to access.), 220, 221
Death, IRA procedures, 23
Disclosure Statement (Document that must be given by an IRA trustee or custodian to IRA holders when the initial IRA agreement is signed. The Disclosure Statement describes the rights of an IRA holder, how money can be transferred, fees charged to the IRA holder, and potential long-term rate of return if the IRA is set up in interest-bearing securities.), 22, 24, 25
Dividends (Payment of a portion of earnings or return on interest to investors. Dividend payments are usually made on a regular schedule, such as quarterly, and the income counts as investment income for tax purposes, rather than capital gains.), 127, 162
  Bond (Interest earned on bonds is returned to investors as bond dividends.), 127
  Coupons (Another term for dividend payments on bonds. At one time bonds came with actual coupons that could be redeemed for payment. Thus, zero-coupon bonds are those without coupons.), 127
  Stock (Many corporations pay portions of their earnings to shareholders as dividends. Generally new and startup companies pay no dividends, opting to keep profits for expansion.), 162
Divorce, IRA Procedures, 23
Dow Jones & Co. (The public corporation that owns the *Wall Street Journal* and *Barron's*, among other things.), 170, 220, 221
Dow Jones Industrial Average/ DJIA (An average made up of 30 stocks, initially formulated to monitor movements of the stock market before the advent of computers.), 167–170
  List of stocks used for DJIA average, 168

FDIC, Federal Deposit Insurance Corporation (A Federal government agency that protects investors—up to $100,000 per institution—against being hurt in the collapse of a bank.), 72–77, 123
Fees and Commissions, IRA, 26, 72–77, 111–112
Financial Planners (People who study the financial situation of an individual and make recommendations for future allotment of money in the form of a financial plan. Financial planner is a generic term and does not guarantee any form of qualification or licensing, in contrast to stockmarket Registered Representatives who must pass a qualifying exam.), 9–11
Forbe's Magazine (A bi-weekly financial magazine owned by the Forbes family.), 2, 163
Futures (*See Commodities Futures.*)

Ginnie Maes, Government National Mortgage Association (*See Bonds*)
Grantor (The official designation for the IRA investor or holder in the Disclosure Statement and other IRA documents executed with the IRA trustee.), 22–25

Income, money earned
   Capital Gains Income (Money earned as a result of the increase in market price of an investment. When the investment is sold, this becomes a realized capital gain, when unsold, it is an unrealized capital gain. Similarly, money lost as a result of the decrease in market price of an investment is a capital loss.), 24, 25, 194–195.
   Investment Income (Money earned from dividends or interest payments from an investment.), 24, 25
   Salary Income (Income obtained in the form of salary, bonuses, or commissions counts as salary income to qualify for IRA treatment.), 24, 25
Individual Retirement Account, IRA (Any form of IRA other than an annuity.), 1
Individual Retirement Annuity, IRA (An IRA obtained through an insurance company.), 36
Individual Retirement Arrangement, IRA (The official name for an IRA as specified by the IRS. Such IRAs include those offered by all institutions including insurers.), 1
Insurance (Protection purchased in exchange for regular payment of premiums that will pay the beneficiary in the event of specific losses of life or money. No insurance benefits may be included in an IRA.), 72–77
Interest Rate (Rate that interest will be earned on a specific investment at the outset of that investment. Interest rates are expressed as a percentage of the initial principal investment.), 129
Investment Income (*See Income*)

Keogh Plan (A retirement investment program structured under tax law similar to an IRA, but for people who are self-employed. A salaried worker with part-time self-employment on the side can have both a Keogh Plan and an IRA.), 84–92

Maturity (The point at which a bond or other debt security becomes due and payable to the investor. Stocks don't have maturity dates.), 32, 33
McGraw-Hill (*See Standard & Poor's*)
Modem (An attachment that ties a computer to the telephone so that information from data banks and other sources can be fed directly into the computer.), 218
Money Market Deposit Accounts (Bank accounts that work like money market funds. They often offer higher rates than savings accounts by investing in the money market, but as a result the rate of return varies as interest rates move up and down.), 31, 128, 129
Municipals (*See Bonds, Municipal*)
Mutual Funds (Large funds set up by advisory companies to invest in many securities that are sold, in the form of small shares, to individual investors. There are mutual funds that invest in most forms of securities from over-the-counter stocks to municipal bonds.), 93–99
   Advisor (Company that employs fund managers who select and purchase securities for the funds. Among mutual funds the advisor is usually also the management company that

INDEX

sets up the fund, sells shares to the public and manages the operations. Neither the advisor nor the manager own the fund, which is owned by the investors who buy the mutual fund shares. In commodities pools—which are a form of mutual fund—the advisor and manager are often separate companies.), 93–99

Families (When a mutual fund advisor or management company offers shares in more than one fund among which an investor can transfer his IRA or other investment with a telephone call. Dozens of mutual fund management companies offer five or more different mutual funds, among which the investor can easily move his money.), 93–99

Index (Index mutual funds buy all the shares in a well-known index like the Standard & Poor's 500, or even all the shares offered on a stock exchange.), 2

Management Companies (*See Mutual Funds, Advisor*)

Money Market (Money market mutual funds invest in money market securities such as Treasury Bills or Commercial Paper. Tax-exempt money market funds invest in short-term paper issues by municipalities.), 128–129

No-load (No-load mutual funds don't charge investors a portion of their investment as a fee when they enter a fund. These funds do charge an annual management fee for managing the money. This annual fee is often a bit higher than that charged by load funds, which often charge 8½% when you buy into the fund.), 94

NASD, National Association of Securities Dealers (A non-profit corporation set up by Congress in 1938 to which all securities dealers and brokers must belong. The NASD is responsible for regulation of the over-the-counter securities market under direction of the Securities & Exchange Commission, a Federal government agency.), 115

NASDAQ, NASD Automatic Quotation System (A computerized system for providing continuous and daily quotations for nearly 5000 over-the-counter stocks directed by the NASD and operated through computers at brokerage trading desks around the country. NASDAQ price quotations for the largest OTC stocks are reprinted in daily newspapers.), 173

Net worth (Net worth of a company is the portion of the assets represented by the owner's actual investment, thus it is sometimes called shareholders' equity or book value. To find net worth on a balance sheet you must go to the bottom of the liabilities column. Since net worth is also the amount by which actual assets exceed actual liabilities, a figure must be entered at the bottom of the liabilities column to make the balance sheet balance. Net worth and net worth per share are considered one way to evaluate public companies.), 162, 188

New York Stock Exchange, NYSE (This is the world's largest auction exchange for stocks. Stocks traded there must qualify for listing—meeting size and other requirements. Brokers buy seats or memberships to buy and sell those stocks for their customers on the floor of the NYSE, which is on Wall Street in Manhattan. There are more than a half dozen other exchanges in the U.S. including the Pacific Stock Exchange, on the West Coast. Some stocks are traded on more than one exchange—dually listed—while others trade entirely off the exchanges—over-the-counter. The NYSE Index includes prices of all the stocks on the NYSE.), 167–170

No-load funds (*See Mutual Funds*)

Options (Option contracts buy an investor the right to purchase a given security at a given price in the future. Option sellers, on the other hand, have the obligation to offer the underlying security or the price amount of the underlying security.), 194–196

    Calls (A call option gives the buyer the right to call-away a stock or other security at a prespecified price in the future, even if the price at that future time is higher than the price-amount of the call option. Thus, you make profits by buying call options on stocks that rise in price. The call seller, on the other hand, must give up his stock at that higher price or pay out the difference to the call buyer.), 194–196

    Puts *See Calls, above* (Put buyers have the right to put a given stock to a put seller at a predetermined price, even if the price of the stock drops below the predetermined level. The put seller, on the other hand, has the obligation to buy that stock at the predetermined higher price or make up the difference even if the market price is below the predetermined level. Thus, you make profits by buying put options on stocks that fall in price.), 194–196

Over-the-Counter (Technically, there is no counter over which you purchase stocks, although decades ago—when securities law was different—you could buy stocks over the counter in many banks. Today this is the designation for stocks or bonds that aren't traded on the big exchanges, or for off-the-exchange trades of stocks that are offered in both places. OTC stocks tend to be smaller than exchange-listed companies and often are new public companies.), 139, 172–180

Par (The face value of a bond. But a bond may be sold—even on the offering date—at a price lower or higher than par, based largely on changes in interest rates between the time the bond offering is announced and when the bonds are actually offered for sale. Thus, a bond may be "priced below par" or "priced above par." *See Yield.*), 129

Penalities, IRA, 18, 21, 79

Portfolio, Investment (A compilation of all of an investor's or fund's investments.), 42–49

P/E Ratio, Price/Earnings Ratio (The ratio of the current market price of a stock to the earnings or net income per share. A stock with a P/E of 10 would have a stock price of 10 times the earnings per share on its income statement.), 162, 187, 188

Prime Rate (The rate commercial banks charge their most credit-worthy corporate customers; thus, the lowest rate at which corporations can borrow.)

Principal (The amount of the actual investment, usually in bonds or money market investments. Principal plus interest and the rate interest is compounded make up the rate of return in the money market and on bonds that are held to maturity. *Also see Capital.*), 163

Prohibited Transactions, IRA, 179

Prospectus (Legal document required by the Securities & Exchange Commission when a security is offered for sale to the public. Certain disclosures are required and the document must be filled with the SEC and given to potential investors on request. The company's legal obligation is to be truthful in the prospectus, and the SEC doesn't rule on investment worth.), 166, 176

Proxy Material (Legal documents required by the SEC when shareholders are to vote on motions, election of board members or other matters. Most companies issue proxy material once each year prior to their annual meeting of stockholders. This information is on file with the SEC and publicly available.)

Puts (*See Options*)

Real Estate, 40, 41, 78, 79, 82, 199

REITS, Real Estate Investment Trusts (Publicly held real estate companies in which shareholders buy stock, often over the stock exchanges. Because these companies are set up as trusts under special law, they must return 95% of their income as dividends to investors.), 40, 41

Return (*See Price, Bond*)

Requirements, IRS, 17–23

Rollovers (In IRAs, the transfer of a sum of money from a mature CD or other investment or from a pension plan into an IRA.), 21, 22

SEC Securities & Exchange Commission (The Federal government agency that oversees all public securities trading.), 114, 166, 176

Shorting, Short Selling (Selling securities in the future that you don't currently own in an attempt to make a profit when the market price drops. The opposite is going long, or buying to make a future profit when the market price rises in the future.), 59, 190–193

SIPC, Securities Investor Protection Corporation (This is a non-profit corporation created by Congress to protect small investors against damage if a brokerage house holding his securities or cash collapses. All brokers contribute to SIPC and share in the insurance it offers investors—up to $100,000 per customer. SIPC isn't a Federal government agency like the FDIC, which similarly protects investors against the collapse of a bank.), 72–77

Spread, between bid and ask, 177

S & P, Standard & Poor (A company that is a subsidiary of McGraw-Hill, which also publishes *Business Week* magazine. Standard & Poor

provides bond ratings and other research on stocks and bonds.), 170
    S & P 500 (The 500 largest stocks followed by Standard & Poor. Options and other investments are often pinned to this index and to the S & P 100, which is a narrower index of larger company stocks.), 2, 161, 162, 167

Tax-exempt Bonds (*See Bonds, Municipals*)
Tax Shelter (Investments that permit investors to avoid paying current taxes, although most will eventually produce either large losses or income that will be taxable. Only municipal bonds provide income that isn't federally taxable currently or in the future, and this may be ended or curtailed in the forthcoming tax reform.), 10
Ten-K, 10-K (The official annual document company must file with the Securities and Exchange Commission in which it must show financial statements for the year and meet other disclosure requirements. *See Annual Report*.), 166, 167
Thrifts, Thrift Institutions (Name frequently used for Savings & Loan Associations and Savings Banks.)
Transferring, IRA Investments, IRA rules, 20, 21
Treasury Securities (*See Bonds, Government*)
Trustee/ IRA (Under the law an IRA must be opened with an institution that qualifies as an IRA trustee or IRA custodian. For the purposes of an IRA holder it doesn't make much difference which is selected, although banks tend to act as trustees while large brokerage houses are generally custodians.)

Unit Trusts (*See Mutual Funds*)

Wall Street Journal (The daily financial newspaper published by Dow Jones & Co.), 2, 163, 170, 186, 212
Withdrawal, IRA, 19, 20

Yield (Yield is what an investor actually will receive if he purchases an investment today in terms of interest. It differs from the interest rate in that yield is affected by frequency of compounding of interest and the price at which a bond is actually purchased. The interest rate on a bond is established when the bond is selling at par, which may not even be the price at which it is sold to investors, let alone the price when it is later trading in secondary markets.), 129
Yield to Maturity (Yield figures quoted in daily newspapers for, as an example, Treasury Notes, are also the "yield to maturity" if you were to acquire them immediately. That means your yield on your investment would remain at that level no matter what yield was quoted for the same Treasury Notes a month later—the price at which you could sell your bond or note would change, but your yield would not. The term is most generally used for municipal bonds, where it means the same thing.), 137–139

Zeros (*See Bonds, Zero-Coupon*)